Alice Through the Looking-Glass

Lewis Carroll's
Alice Through the
Looking-Glass

adapted for the stage by

James Reaney

The Porcupine's Quill, Inc.

CANADIAN CATALOGUING IN PUBLICATION DATA

Reaney, James, 1926-
Lewis Carroll's Alice through the looking-glass

A play.
ISBN 0-88984-147-0

I. Carroll, Lewis, 1832-1898.
Through the looking-glass.
II. Title.
III. Title: Alice through the looking-glass.

PS8535.E24L4 1994   C812'.54   C94-931671-7
PR9199.3.R43L4 1994

Published by The Porcupine's Quill, Inc.,
68 Main Street, Erin, Ontario NOB 1TO
with financial assistance from
The Canada Council and the Ontario Arts Council.
The support of the Government of Ontario
through the Ministry of Culture, Tourism and Recreation
is also gratefully acknowledged.

Represented in Canada by the Literary Press Group.
Trade orders available from General Distribution Services.

Readied for the press by Michael Carbert.
Copy edited by Doris Cowan.

For performance information please contact
Cultural Support Services Inc., (416) 962-6200,
P.O. Box 190, 260 Adelaide St. East, Toronto,
Ontario M4X 1M3, Canada.

Contents

Preface

AFTER WRITING *Alice's Adventures in Wonderland* for the six-year-old girl next door, Alice Liddell, the Reverend Charles Lutwidge Dodgson, who wrote under the name 'Lewis Carroll', waited five or six years before writing a sequel, *Through the Looking-Glass and What Alice Found There*. Now, the fact that Alice Liddell was fast approaching eleven years of age may have influenced the shape of the new story. It starts out with Alice in a chess game playing the part of a very young pawn who in five or more moves arrives at the other end of the board as a Queen, more grown-up and more like twelve than the eleven and a half she says she is at the beginning of the story, and certainly a long way from the six-year-old girl who once was Alice in Wonderland. Well, if you listen carefully, you will note that in the beginning of *Through the Looking-Glass*, Alice is very much bossed around by the adult figures, in particular the Red Queen, who is said to be based on Miss Prickle, Alice's governess in real life. However, increasingly as the story flows along, Alice is less subservient until, at the very end, it is she who is ordering both the Red and the White Queen around. Are we not watching the growing up of a child into an independent young lady who has learned a great deal from surviving so many encounters with strange people and situations, all of which she has addressed with a politeness and civility most of us would find very hard to manage? And without seeming to, Alice had also learnt much to think about in the years to come. She may very well spend the rest of her life completely impervious to boredom. Who could be bored after confronting such conundrums as 'whether pigs have wings', whether her dream about the Red King asleep in Looking-glass Land has been dreamed by herself or she is herself a phantom in the Red King's

MERVYN BLAKE RED KING

dream? You'll meet his drowsy Majesty on Square Four where Tweedledum and Tweedledee announce the cheerful fact that if the Red King wakes up from his dream about Alice, she may go out like a candle!

Some of you are murmuring that you do not know how to play chess. Do not fret. You probably know how to play checkers which is a simplified version of chess. In both games, sixteen white pieces contest sixteen red, or black pieces for ownership of a board marked out in thirty-two white squares and thirty-two red ones. With one exception, Alice moves across this board one square at a time, and it always seems to be her move. Note that whenever she makes a move there is a lightning-swift change of place; imagine what you would feel like if you were a checker and some big hand picked you up and, suddenly, you were somewhere else you'd never seen before. Therefore, one moment Alice is in the Garden of Live Flowers, the next moment she is on a train moving swiftly over Square Three to land on Square Four.

A great many people go through life without questioning the sanity of the way our genetics and our society and our minds arrange things – left is left and right is right; first you prick your finger with a pin, and next you scream. But suppose you lived in a looking-glass world like the White Queen's where everything was the other way around – left was right and right was left. With an orange in one hand, take a look at yourself in the mirror and you'll see at once where Carroll got the idea for the whole story. The orange you hold in your right hand now, in the looking-glass, appears to be in your left hand; so, perhaps, in the reflective world, you would scream first and then prick your finger; perhaps you would be first imprisoned, then sentenced for a crime that you will not commit until tomorrow. Why? Because in Looking-glass Land time flows backward. Could this ever be so? Yes, it is so every time a great artist such as Lewis Carroll gets tired of our always predictable world and decides to liven things up a bit by suggesting other possibilities. Why should we always be content with the same boring routines day after day? And perhaps too, they will be more bearable for the refreshment we have been given in the new things we find out about when we too pass through the Looking-glass.

Carroll's first *Alice* book released its readers from boredom by taking them to 'Wonderland'. Actually, the original title was 'Alice's Adventures *Underground*' [italics mine]. I think then what happened is that Carroll pondered how he could turn the world upside down another way and so invented a world where Alice would have adventures *under water*. At one point, near the end of the tale, Alice opines that all of the poetry she has heard in Looking-glass Land seems to be about fishes, and, of course, like a looking-glass, water reflects images the other way around and also contains strange fish creatures (whales and octopuses, for example) who have a submarine dream-like feeling about them. Anything seems to be possible under water, even eels who have developed electric batteries!

Long before it was thought of, Lewis Carroll was a practitioner of Surrealism – the Salvador Dali world of melting, bent watches and fur-lined teacups. Also, Carroll is the first in a long line of Oxford University eccentrics who have strongly urged us to abandon this boring, humdrum world for something more interesting, such as Tolkien's Hobbit Shire or C.S. Lewis's Narnia.

One of my favourite lines in the story is Alice's remark just after she gets through the looking-glass into the room *behind* it: 'They certainly don't keep this room as tidy as the other.' In view of the fully active railway train, the deer in the Forest of Namelessness, and the Egg balanced precariously on a wall as well as the four thousand or so soldiers kept by the White King – all things a cleaning lady might object to – this has to be the understatement of the nineteenth century.

Still, may we all, in our soul, have such an untidy room!

James Reaney

Foreword

AS I REMEMBER IT, it was some time early in 1991 when David William, then artistic director of the Stratford Festival, suggested that Reaney, because he was a poet, might be able to adapt *Through the Looking-Glass and What Alice Found There* and succeed where other non-poet adaptors had failed. In 1965, Mr William had directed my first play, *The Killdeer,* and so had experienced my poetic fury at close range.

Who could refuse the chance to work on such an enchanting story in which a small girl (not unlike Anne Shirley, who also is always questioning) dives into a mirror over a fireplace and in so doing challenges reality as we know it; for behind the looking-glass an absurd chess game is in progress where all our normal time/space clichés are exuberantly turned upside down. I found out, in my research, that Lewis Carroll, forbidden by Alice's parents to enter their house ever again, had written *Looking-Glass* as a farewell to his dream-girl for whom he had already written another masterpiece – *Alice in Wonderland.* In the second Alice book, Alice floats down an underground river with a Sheep; in the first book, she floated down the Isis at Oxford in full sunlight. My first

---

LEWIS CARROLL was not only fond of telling his stories to children, he was also fond of putting them on – usually with the assistance of magic lantern slides. When both the Alice stories became smash hits on the London stage, he was there hovering over every dissolving view and supervising such inventions as a Humpty Dumpty made out of a barrel with moveable hoops for its mouth. If you feel like following suit – that is, putting on *Alice Through the Looking-Glass* yourself in a penny production – turn to the back pages of this book for some notions on how to do a home-made version.

lesson as an adaptor was that we couldn't show the underground river scene (too expensive) and so had to figure out some substitute, suitably dark and representing a turning point. That's why Jabberwocky has been moved from first thing after the leap through the mirror to the end of Act One where it serves as a reminder that Alice can conquer the Looking-glass monsters, grow up, even get rid of Carroll? I think that if I were adapting the story for the Peking Opera or some other Oriental theatre, an inexpensive boat scene might have been possible, but the patron knows best and, in this case, the model followed is that of nineteenth century Victorian productions of the Alice stories with magic tricks and dissolving views all on dry land. Mind you, Esther Williams could have done it! The other thing I had to give up was directly suggesting the Oxford world behind the Alice books which are very much in a tradition that goes back to Friar Bacon and Duns Scotus and forward to Gerard Manley Hopkins, C.S. Lewis, and J.R.R. Tolkien – eccentric, donnish, obsessed with fantastic 'elsewheres' quite unlike our couch-potato kitchen-sink scenarios. That's o.k.; anyone with half a glim can see that the White Knight is the Professor oxoniensis *mirabilis, eccentricus, mens vacuus*.

At first, the production seemed headed for the Third Stage acted by the Young Company and so experiment seemed called for; e.g., why not bring on Lewis Carroll himself producing the story with magic lantern slides as he often did when entertaining children, and also not only show the prototype for the White Knight but also show Alice's mother and father, the Liddells, who seem to be the Red Queen and Humpty Dumpty, perhaps one of the reasons they locked Carroll out of their house?

What intervened here was the effect of the late Elliott Hayes's adaptation of Robertson Davies's *Fifth Business*, a big hit at Stratford the year this project started. It is the story of a small boy, Paul Dempster, who falls through the mirror of illusions and never gets back, becoming in the process a world-famous magician, capable of making everyone happy save himself. Magic effects have to abound here, and I soon sensed that furthering this trend with the Alice show might be part of a Stratford tradition. A couple of nights ago I watched Tom Baxter, the magic advisor for the show, make a salt shaker disappear at the Keystone Café as well as bend a spoon without bending it, and it's irresistible to have a show that can do that on a grand scale. My director, Marti Maraden, has also recently directed *Love's Labour's Lost* at Stratford wherein donnish intellectuals hide from the world in a tree house. It must have been a natural move for her to next direct not only Corneille's *L'Illusion comique* but to go on to a story involving a White Knight who long ago had hidden himself in the Looking-glass learnèd labyrinths of Oxford, where he was willing to guide a child visitor in and out of that fantastic mirror world of wonders towards a début of growing maturity back in the 'real' world.

So, as the preparatory workshop with the Young Company started in the fall of 1992, my adaption had pretty well shaken down into its present shape except that a great deal of my commentary and suggestions were kept as part of the rehearsed reading shown to Richard Monette and David William and invited guests so that I myself actually read out my mental landscapes of *Looking-glass* in fear and trembling since the many rewrites and keeping this and dropping that produced land-mines for cues.

Donna (Choreographer) arranging Dum & Dee

With great fondness I remember Marcel Jeannin's White Knight. A young French-Canadian actor, he fell off his horse (rehearsal chair) with great abandon and chivalric devotion. You really believed he adored Alice, and in the true spirit of the book, he seemed a demented Don Quixote willing to tilt at any windmill that threatened his beloved Dulcinea-Alicia. Mr Monette took to the story as played that night in late October and also to its trajectory away from Third Stage to the Avon with a cast of seasoned Stratford actors – Douglas Rain as Humpty, Barbara Bryne as the White Queen, both actors who had in 1967 appeared in my first Stratford play, *Colours in the Dark*.

And so there has come about the fabulous, magic, fairy-tale production you are about to see, or read. Slowly it has begun to slide from the drawing board to the stage of a theatre known in my boyhood as the Majestic, an Ambrose Small theatre, home of Chaplin on tour and the Marx Brothers. In the thirties and early forties it was also where I saw four favourite films: *David Copperfield*, *Snow White and the Seven Dwarfs*, *The Constant Nymph* (Joan Fontaine), and Hitchcock's *Spellbound* – parts of all of which have somehow crept into my adaptation of the show. Watch Alice (Sarah Polley) in her first encounter with the Fawn in the Forest of Namelessness – that's Snow White meeting the Deer just before she comes upon the Dwarfs' little house.

It's always been great fun working with Marti Maraden on the adaptation and also watching her direct the warm-hearted rehearsals that started up on April 25, 1993. I can't recall a first read-through where there were so many belly laughs and whoops of recognition as an extremely well chosen cast tore into the hilarious procession of grotesques that Carroll has lined up on his magic chessboard of the soul. Centred and foiled are they too by the exquisite rightness of Sarah Polley's casting and performance which brings to the story, as I've remarked above, a feeling of L.M. Montgomery's young innocents from the looking-glass farm-houses and villages of Prince Edward Island.

I am very proud to have helped with such a delightful show with designers, magician, composer, actors, director, and backstage staff who have seen to it that Carroll's magic text and verbal wit is made all the more powerful by their expert ministrations. I well know how a story can drown in overly generous production; not in this case. In the end, led by a wise director, served by sensitive artists, *Alice Through the Looking-Glass* is an actors' triumph cavorting in a verbal furnace fuelled by one of the most quoted authors in the world and backed up by a rich visual and musical wonderland.

James Reaney

P.S. I would also like to thank the children and young people of Stratford itself, with whom, starting in the New Year, I conducted Alice workshops in order to raise Alice fever and increase their enjoyment of the show. These workshops were held at Central Collegiate, King Lear, and Juliet schools, and at the Stratford Museum (King and Douro streets).

RED

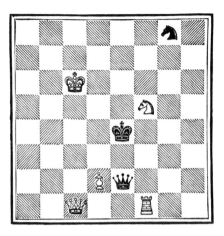

WHITE

White Pawn (Alice) to play, and win in eleven moves.

Alice Through the Looking-Glass

The Workshop Cast

Workshop – September 23-26, 1992
Reading – September 27, 1992

Performed by the 1992 Young Company

GNAT, TIGER LILY, OYSTER, PUDDING,
Tom Allison
TWEEDLEDEE, James Binkley
FATHER (in Jabberwocky),
CARPENTER, OLD MAN (White Knight's Poem), RED KNIGHT,
Scott Fisher
HATTA (Mad Hatter), LARKSPUR, GOAT, Murray Furrow
WHITE KING, ROSE, MESSENGER (in Humpty Dumpty's Poem),
Alain Goulem
UNICORN, SECOND DAISY, GUARD, OYSTER,
Neil Ingram
WHITE KNIGHT, WHITE PAPER GENTLEMAN,
Marcel Jeannin
RED QUEEN, FIRST DAISY, Daria Martel
WHITE QUEEN, Yanna McIntosh
LION, HORSE, WALRUS and NARRATOR/DODGSON,
Mervon Mehta
HUMPTY DUMPTY, Scott Nichol
HAIGHA (Hare), FAWN, BEETLE, Michael Simpson
ALICE, Helen Taylor
TWEEDLEDUM, Dathan B. Williams

DIRECTOR, Marti Maraden
STAGE MANAGER, Ann Stuart

The Avon Cast

Alice Through the Looking-Glass
was originally commissioned by the Stratford Festival Foundation
under the artistic directorship of David William.

ALICE, Sarah Polley
WHITE QUEEN, Barbara Bryne
RED QUEEN, Michelle Fisk
WHITE KING, William Needles
RED KING, Mervyn Blake
WHITE KNIGHT, Tom Wood
TIGER LILY, Donna Starnes
ROSE, Rose Graham
DAISIES,
Gabrielle Jones, Christina Gordon, Lina Giornofelice, Geoffrey Whynot
LARKSPUR, Melanie Janzen
GUARD, Bradley C. Rudy
WHITE PAPER GENTLEMAN, Graham Harley
GOAT, Jeffrey Prentice
BEETLE, Gabrielle Jones
HORSE, Brian Brockenshire
GNAT, Douglas Rain
FAWN, Donna Starnes
TWEEDLEDUM, Bernard Hopkins
TWEEDLEDEE, Keith Dinicol
THE WALRUS, Douglas Rain
THE CARPENTER, Douglas Chamberlain
JABBERWOCKY FATHER, Graham Harley
JABBERWOCKY SON, Geoffrey Whynot
JABBERWOCK, Jeffrey Prentice
HUMPTY DUMPTY, Douglas Rain
RED KNIGHT, Brian Brockenshire
MESSENGER, Mark Harapiak
HAIGHA, Douglas Chamberlain

HATTA, Bradley C. Rudy
UNICORN, Graham Harley
LION, Keith Dinicol
AGED MAN, Mervyn Blake.

Castles, Pawns, Clock, Pictures, Oysters, Stars,
Fingerposts, Soldiers, Knights' Horses, Waiters,
Dinner Party Guests:
Vince Fera, Timothy French, Bradley Garrick, Mark Harapiak,
Robert Yeretch, Edward Daranyi and Members of the Company.

DIRECTOR, Marti Maraden
SET DESIGN, Stephen Britton Osler
COSTUME DESIGN, John Pennoyer
MUSIC, Keith Thomas
LIGHTING DESIGN, Kevin Fraser
SOUND DESIGN, John Hazen
ASSISTANT TO THE DIRECTOR, Donna Starnes
CHOREOGRAPHY, Donna Starnes
MAGIC, Thomas Baxter
MOVEMENT, Wendy Lehr
STAGE MANAGER, Marylu Moyer
ASSISTANT STAGE MANAGERS, Laurie Hirst, Corinne Richards
REHEARSAL STAGE MANAGER, Theresa Malek
PRODUCTION STAGE MANAGER, Hilary Graham
FIGHT DIRECTOR, John Stead
ASSISTANT LIGHTING DESIGNER, Elizabeth Asselstine.

Act One

Alice Through the Looking Glass
Stratford Festival '94
The Walrus

1. Looking-Glass House

Alice, as the curtain rises, is revealed sitting on the carpet looking at the fire and holding a ball of wool which the black kitten keeps getting away on her. A window is startingly white with snow falling and wind blowing outside. The fire in the fireplace has a similar hallucinatory red about it; these colours foreshadow the dream chess game.

Lights come up on a surreal chess board at the back of the stage behind scrim whose pieces (and moves) are limited to those on the diagram furnished by Carroll just after his author's preface (Red Knight, White Knight, White Pawn, White King and Queen, White Castle). Carroll's opening narration is divided thus:

WHITE QUEEN
One thing was certain, that the *white* kitten had had nothing to do with it –

RED QUEEN
It was the black kitten's fault entirely –

WHITE KING
For the white kitten had been having its face washed by the old cat for the last quarter of an hour –

RED KING [*Sleepily*]
And bearing it pretty well, considering.

WHITE KNIGHT
So you see that it couldn't have had any hand in the mischief.

Alice has her wool wound up, the black kitten gets it

away on her and it unwinds. Alice winds up the yarn and
settles down again with the kitten.

ALICE

Do you know, I was so angry, Kitty, when I saw all the mischief you had been doing, I was very nearly opening the window and putting you out into the snow! [*Music that preludes the threshold to another world*] What have you got to say for yourself? Now, don't interrupt me! *Music.* Kitty, can you play chess? Now, don't smile, my dear; I'm asking it seriously. Because when we were playing just now, you watched just as if you understood it and when I said 'Check!' you purred!

   Kitty, dear, let's pretend that you're the Red Queen! [*Reaching for the Red Queen chess piece*] Do you know, I think if you sat up and folded your arms, you'd look exactly like her. Now do try, there's a dear! [*Alice tries to make the kitten do so*] Kitty, because you won't fold your arms properly, I'm going to hold you up to the looking-glass to see how sulky and naughty you are, and if you're not good directly, I'll put you through into Looking-glass House. How would you like *that*?

Alice holds the kitten up to the looking-glass above the fireplace.

ALICE

Now, if you'll only attend, Kitty ... there's the room you can see through the glass that's just the same as our drawing room, only the things go the other way. I can see all of it when I get up on a chair – all but the bit just behind the fireplace. Oh! I do so wish I could see *that* bit! I want so much to know whether they've a fire in the winter. Well then, the books are something like our books, only the words go the wrong way, because I've held up one of our books to the glass, and then they hold up one in the other room.

Oh, Kitty, how nice it would be if we could only get through into Looking-glass House! Let's pretend there's a way of getting through into it. [*She starts to clamber up onto the mantel*] Let's pretend the glass has got all soft like gauze, so that we can get through. Why, it's turning into a sort of mist now. I declare! It'll be easy enough to get through –

She gets up onto the mantel. Music. The fireplace swivels and we proceed to the other side which is a copy of the Liddells' hearth with small changes. There might be a slight struggle as if the Looking-glass world is pushing or pulling her. We then see Alice coming through the glass and after a pause jumping down lightly and nimbly onto the 'other room's' floor. Music and a flash of light.

ALICE [*Sees fire blazing brightly*]
So I shall be as warm here as I was in the old room, warmer in fact, because there'll be no one to scold me away from the fire. Oh, what fun it will be when they see me through the glass in here and can't get at me!

Alice sees the pictures on the wall which are alive! The clock on the Looking-glass chimney grins at her. And she notices a chessboard with pieces which appear to be moving.

ALICE
Here are the Red King and the Red Queen [*In a whisper*] and there are the White King and the White Queen holding her baby, the pawn. And here are two castles walking arm in arm!

ALICE [*Picks up the White King (or Red Queen)*]
Oh! Please don't make such faces, my dear! You make me laugh so I can hardly hold you!

Alice sets the chesspiece gently down on the board. She picks up a book she finds on a table, tries to read, holds it various ways.

ALICE
Why, it's all in some language I don't know.

She holds up a rather largish page on which we see the first verse of Jabberwocky printed backwards. First appearance of the Jabberwock.

ALICE
Why, it's a Looking-glass book, of course! And, if I hold it up to a glass, the words will all go the right way again.

We now see the first verse of Jabberwocky the 'right way'.

> 'Twas brillig, and the slithy toves
> Did gyre and gimble in the wabe:
> All mimsy were the borogoves,
> And the mome raths outgrabe.

Head of Jabberwock floats through the air.
In the following speech, people are whispering as if they were speaking in a stiff-gentle breeze: 'Look at the garden! Look at the garden!' *Diminuendo and crescendo this.*

ALICE
It seems very pretty, but it's *rather* hard to understand! Somehow it seems to fill my head with ideas – only I don't exactly know what they are! But oh! if I don't make haste, I shall have to go back through the Looking-glass before I've seen what the rest of the house is like. Let's have a look at the garden first! [*Pause*] I should see the garden far better if I could get to the top of that hill. And – and here's a path that leads straight to it. At least, no, it doesn't do *that* – [*Sharp turns*] – but I suppose it will at last. But how

curiously it twists! It's more like a corkscrew than a path! Well, *this* goes to the hill, I suppose – no, it doesn't! [*House confronts her*] This goes straight back to the house!

Now she is in the midst of a bed of flowers, tiger lilies etc.

2. The Garden of Live Flowers

ALICE
O Tiger lily! I *wish* you could talk!

TIGER LILY
We *can* talk, when there's anybody worth talking to.

ALICE
Flowers talk?

TIGER LILY
As well as *you* can. And a great deal louder.

ROSE
It isn't manners for us to begin, you know, and I really was
wondering when you'd speak! Said I to myself: 'Her face
has got *some* sense in it, though it's not a clever one!'

TIGER LILY
If only her petals were curled up a little more, she'd be all
right.

ALICE
Aren't you sometimes frightened at being planted out
here, with nobody to take care of you?

ROSE
There's the tree in the middle. What else is it good for?

ALICE
But what could it do if any danger came?

ROSE
It could bark.

DAISY
It says Bough-wough! That's why its branches are called boughs.

ANOTHER DAISY
Didn't you know that?

ALL THE FLOWERS [*Ad lib*]

TIGER LILY
Silence, every one of you! They know I can't get at them or they wouldn't dare to do it!

ALICE
Never mind! [*Stooping down over the daisies*] If you don't hold your tongues, I'll pick you!

The daisies are silent. Some redden.

TIGER LILY
That's right! Those daisies are the worst of all. When one speaks, they all begin together and it's enough to make one wither to hear the *way* they go on.

ALICE
Are there any more people in the garden besides me?

ROSE
There's one other flower in the garden that can move about like you. I wonder how you do it –

TIGER LILY
You're always wondering.

ROSE
– but she's more bushy than you are.

ALICE
Is she like me?

ROSE
Well, she has the same awkward shape as you, but she's redder – and her petals are shorter, I think.

TIGER LILY
They're done up close, like a dahlia, not tumbled about like yours.

ROSE [*Kindly*]
But that's not *your* fault. You're beginning to fade, you know, and then one can't help one's petals getting a little untidy.

ALICE
Does she ever come out here?

ROSE
I dare say you'll see her soon. She's one of the kind that has nine spikes, you know.

ALICE
Where does she wear them?

LARKSPUR
She's coming. I can hear her footstep, thump, thump, along the gravel-walk.

We should hear this sound as the Red Queen (full size) comes into view.

ALICE
The Red Queen! [*Pause*]
She's grown a great deal!

ROSE
It's the fresh air that does it.

ALICE
I think I'll go and meet her.

ROSE
You can't possibly do that. *I* should advise you to walk the other way.

What Alice does not realize is that the Red Queen, as well as a great many other things and people, is only seen reflected in some sort of mirror that in Looking-glass Land produces the illusion that someone behind you is really in front of you; therefore, if you move forwards you are actually moving away from the person.

Alice goes up to the Red Queen, but she retreats and disappears. Then Alice backs up, goes the other way to extreme stage left and bumps into the lady.

3. Alice Meets Red Queen

RED QUEEN [*The concentrated essence of all gover-nesses, a controlled formal fury*] Where do you come from? And where are you going? Look up, speak nicely, and don't twiddle your fingers all the time.

ALICE [*Obeying instructions to the letter*]
I've lost my way.

RED QUEEN
I don't know what you mean by *your* way: all the ways about here belong to *me* –but why did you come out here at all? Curtsey while you're thinking what to say. It saves time.

ALICE [*Aside*]
I'll try it when I go home, the next time I'm a little late for dinner.

RED QUEEN
It's time for you to answer now; open your mouth a *little* wider when you speak, and always say 'your Majesty.'

ALICE
I only wanted to see what the garden was like, your Majesty –

RED QUEEN [*Patting her head*]
That's right: although, when you say 'garden' – *I've* seen gardens, compared with which this would be a wilderness.

ALICE
And I thought I'd try and find my way to the top of that hill –

RED QUEEN
When you say hill, *I* could show you a hill, in comparison with which you'd call that a valley.

ALICE
No, I shouldn't: a hill can't be a valley, you know. That would be nonsense!

RED QUEEN [*Shaking her head*]
You may call it 'nonsense' if you like, but *I've* heard nonsense compared with which that would be as sensible as a dictionary!

Alice curtseys and in silence they walk up the little hill. When they reach the top, we can see what they see.

ALICE
I declare it's marked out just like a large chessboard! There ought to be some men moving about somewhere – and so there are! It's a great huge game of chess that's being played – all over the world – if this *is* the world at all, you know. Oh, what fun it is! How I *wish* I was one of them! I wouldn't mind being a Pawn, if only I might join – though of course I should *like* to be a Queen, best.

RED QUEEN [*Picking up pointer*]
That's easily managed. You can be the White Queen's Pawn, if you like; and you're in the Second Square to begin with. [*She points this out on backdrop and also touches other points of interest in Alice's White Pawn corridor*] When you get to the Eighth Square you'll be a Queen. Run! _____ !!!

Running: this requires some sort of escalator treadmill belt. One thing we should notice is that the runners never get past the hill and tree.

RED QUEEN
Faster! Faster!

ALICE [*Aside*]
But we never seem to pass anything. I wonder if all the things move along with us?

RED QUEEN
Faster! Don't try to talk. Faster! Faster!

ALICE [*After a while*]
Are we nearly there?

RED QUEEN
Nearly there! Why, we passed it ten minutes ago! Faster! [*The wind whistles. Alice's hair is blown back*]   Now! Now! Faster! Faster!

At length, the running and the treadmill slow down and wobble. After Alice has dropped to the ground, she and the Red Queen get off the treadmill. The Red Queen, panting, props Alice up against the tree.

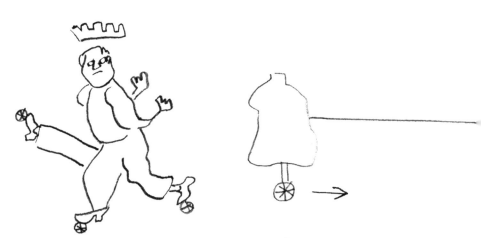

White Queen Running

RED QUEEN
You may rest a little, now.

ALICE
Why, I do believe we've been under this tree the whole
time! Everything's – [*Breathless pause*] – just as it was!

RED QUEEN
Of course it is. What would you have it?

ALICE
Well, in *our* country, you'd generally get to somewhere
else – if you ran very fast for a long time as we've been
doing.

RED QUEEN
A slow sort of country! Now, *here*, you see, it takes all the
running *you* can do, to keep in the same place. If you want
to get somewhere else, you must run at least twice as fast
as that.

ALICE
I'd rather not try, please! I'm quite content to stay here –
only I *am* so hot and thirsty!

RED QUEEN
I know what *you'd* like! Have a biscuit?

*Alice cautiously accepts a large biscuit produced from
the Queen's pocket in a small box. Her face crumples up
with the effort not to choke as she tries to eat it.*

RED QUEEN
While you're refreshing yourself, I'll just take the measure-
ments. [*With measuring tape produced from pocket, she
measures the ground*] At the end of two yards I shall give
you your directions – have another biscuit?

ALICE
No, thank you; one's quite enough!

RED QUEEN
Thirst quenched, I hope? Pawn goes two squares in its first move, you know. So you'll go very quickly through the Third Square – by railway, I should think – and you'll find yourself in the Fourth Square in no time … Well, that square belongs to Tweedledum and Tweedledee – the Fifth Square is mostly water – the Sixth Square, Humpty Dumpty. But you make no remark?

ALICE
I – I didn't know I had to make one – just then.

RED QUEEN
You *should* have said: 'It's extremely kind of you to tell me all this' – however, we'll suppose it said – the Seventh Square is all forest – however, one of the Knights will show you the way – and in the Eighth Square we shall be Queens together, and it's all feasting and fun!
    Speak in French when you can't think of the English for a thing. Turn out your toes as you walk and remember who you are! Goodbye!   [*Red Queen exits, but leaves a note which Alice picks up and reads*]

ALICE
'White Pawn' (Alice) to play, and win in eleven moves.

4. White Pawn to Play: Through Square Three by Railway

Out of the surrounding darkness suddenly appears the railway compartment, filled with its surreal company of Horse, Goat, Beetle, Gentleman dressed in white paper and others. Just before the move begins we should hear the brook. Next, a really loud train whistle, sound of train rushing up, darkness as Alice disappears, then light up on the railway compartment where Alice finds herself in strange company.

GUARD
Tickets, please! Now then! Show your ticket, child!

CHORUS
Don't keep him waiting child! Why, his time is worth a thousand pounds a minute!

ALICE
I'm afraid I haven't got one. There wasn't a ticket-office where I came from.

CHORUS
There wasn't room for one where she came from. The land there is worth a thousand pounds an inch!

GUARD
Don't make excuses. You should have bought one from the engine-driver.

CHORUS
The man that drives the engine. Why, the smoke alone is worth a thousand pounds a puff!

ALICE [*Aside*]
Then there's no use in speaking –

CHORUS
Better say nothing at all. Language is worth a thousand pounds a word!

ALICE
I shall dream about a thousand pounds tonight. I know I shall.

Guard uses opera glasses to examine the child.

GUARD:
You're travelling the wrong way. [*Shuts window, exits*]

WHITE PAPER GENT
So young a child ought to know which way she is going, even if she doesn't know her own name!

GOAT [*Bleating*]
She ought to know her way to the ticket office, even if she doesn't know her alphabet.

BEETLE [*With very gentle voice*]
She'll have to go back from here as luggage!

HORSE
Change engines. [*Chokes, ceases talking*]

ALICE [*Aside*]
It sounds like a horse.

GNAT
You might make a joke on that – something about horse and 'hoarse', as in the phrase 'hoarse voice', you know.

BEETLE
She must be labelled 'Lass, handle with care,' you know.

ALICE
What a number of people there are in the carriage.

GOAT
She must be sent as a message by the telegraph.

HORSE
She must draw the train herself, the rest of the way.

PAPER GENT
Never mind what they all say, my dear, but take a return ticket every time the train stops.

ALICE
Indeed, I shan't. I don't belong to this railway journey at all – I was in a wood just now – and I wish I could get back there!

GNAT   [*At this point he is invisible but his amplified voice is heard on loudspeakers*]
You might make a joke on that. Something about you *would* if you could, you know.

ALICE
Don't tease so. If you're so anxious to have a joke made, why don't you make one yourself?

Shrill whistle.
Everyone jumps up in alarm.

HORSE   [*With head out of window, then in*]
It's only a brook we have to jump over.
[*We hear the brook sound*]

ALICE

Should a train try to jump? However, it'll take us into the Fourth Square, that's some comfort!

Compartment angles up and in the confusion Alice catches hold of the Goat's beard. Sound of a train jumping, shuddery moment, sudden change to Alice sitting beneath a tree with insect on twig above her.

5. Conversation with a Gnat

Gnat gives a deep sigh.

ALICE
If only it would sigh like other people.

GNAT
I know you are a friend and you won't hurt me though I *am* an insect.

ALICE
What kind of insect?

GNAT
What, then, you don't –

ALICE [*Aside*]
Why, it's a Gnat, about the size of a chicken! Certainly a very large gnat.

GNAT
Then you don't like *all* insects?

ALICE
I like them when they can talk. None of them ever talk, where I come from.

GNAT
Well, what sort of insects do you rejoice in where *you* come from?

ALICE
I don't *rejoice* in insects at all because I'm rather afraid of them – at least the large kinds. But I can tell you the

names of some of them.

GNAT
Of course they answer to their names?

ALICE
I never knew them to do it.

GNAT
What's the use of their having names if they won't answer
to them?

ALICE
No use to *them*. But it is useful to the people that name
them, I suppose. If not, why do things have names at all?

GNAT
I can't say. Further on, in the wood down there, they've
got no names – however, go on with your list of insects:
you're wasting time.

ALICE
Well, there's the Horse-fly.

GNAT
All right. Hmm. Halfway up that bush you'll see a
Rocking-horse-fly, if you look. It's made entirely of wood,
and gets about by swinging itself from branch to branch.

ALICE
What does it live on?

GNAT
Sap and sawdust. Go on with the list.

ALICE
And then there is the Butterfly.

GNAT

Crawling at your feet you may observe a Bread-and-Butter-fly. Its wings are thin slices of bread-and-butter, its body is a crust, and its head is a lump of sugar.

ALICE

And what does it live on?

GNAT

Weak tea with cream in it.

ALICE

Supposing it couldn't find any?

GNAT

Then it would die, of course.

ALICE

But that must happen very often.

GNAT

It always happens. [*Flies about humming, then settles on a branch*] I suppose you don't want to lose your name. And yet I don't know. Only think how convenient it would be if you could manage to go home without it! For instance, if the governess wanted to call you to your lessons, she would call out 'Come here – ' and there she would have to leave off because there wouldn't be any name for her to call, and of course, you wouldn't have to go, you know.

ALICE

That would never do, I'm sure. The governess would never think of excusing me lessons for that. If she couldn't remember my name, she'd call me 'Miss', as the servants do.

GNAT

Well, if she said 'Miss', and didn't say anything more, of course you'd *miss* your lessons.   [*Pause*]   That's a joke. I wish *you* had made it.

ALICE

Why do you wish *I* had made it? It's a very bad joke. [*Gnat weeps, sighs*]   You shouldn't make jokes if it makes you so unhappy.

Gnat sighs, vanishes, perhaps with a little trail of amplified sighs fading away through the auditorium.

6. The Wood of Namelessness

Alice shivers, gets up and walks off. Immediately, the Wood of Namelessness appears. Rustling and gothic horrid-wood noises. The Jabberwock's eyes appear above the trees.

ALICE

This looks much darker than the last wood. [*Pause*] However, I certainly can't go back. It is the only way to the Eighth Square. This must be the wood where things have no names. I wonder what'll become of my name when I go in? I shouldn't like to lose it at all – because they'd have to give me another, and it would be almost certain to be an ugly one. But then the fun would be, trying to find the creature that had got my old name! Just fancy calling everything you met 'Alice!' till one of them answered. Then, I'd say, 'That's my name. I want it back.' [*She enters the wood*] Well, at any rate, it's a great comfort after being so hot, to get into the – into the – into *what*? I mean to get under the – under the – under *this*, you know! [*We see her place her hand on a tree trunk*] What does it call itself, I wonder? [*Pause*] I do believe it's got no name – why, to be sure it hasn't. [*Pause*] Then it really *has* happened, after all! And now who am I? I *will* remember, if I can! I'm determined to do it! [*Pause*] L. I *know* it begins with L! [*Enter a fawn*] Here then! Here then! [*Holds out hand, Fawn shies away, then allows Alice to stroke her*]

FAWN

What do you call yourself?

ALICE

Nothing. I wish I knew. Nothing just now.

FAWN
Think again. That won't do.

ALICE [*Pause*]
Please, would you tell me what you call yourself? I think
that might help a little.

FAWN
I'll tell you, if you'll come a little further on. I can't
remember here.

*But the wood does not give in very easily as it shifts this
way and that until the fawn breaks out in centre stage
and comes towards us.*

FAWN
I'm a Fawn! And dear me, you're a human child.

Suddenly alarmed, the fawn darts away.

ALICE
Well, at least I know my name now, that's *some* comfort.
Alice – Alice – I won't forget it again.

*She sees two finger posts pointing the same way, one
marked to Tweedledum's house and the other to the
house of Tweedledee.*

And now, which of these posts ought I to follow, I wonder?
[*Walks on*] I do believe that they live in the *same* house! I
wonder I never thought of that before. But I can't stay there
long. I'll just call and say 'How d'ye do?' and ask them the
way out of the wood. If I could only get to the Eighth Square
before it gets dark. [*She turns around to discover two
identical fat little men and spots the labels they bear on
their collars, 'Dum' and 'Dee'*] I suppose they've each got
'Tweedle' round at the back of the collar.

7. Tweedledum & Tweedledee

DUM

If you think we're waxworks, you ought to pay, you know. Waxworks weren't made to be looked at for nothing. Nohow!

DEE

Contrariwise, if you think we're alive, you ought to speak.

ALICE

I'm sure I'm very sorry. [*She recites*]

> Tweedledum and Tweedledee
>   Agreed to have a battle;
> For Tweedledum said Tweedledee
>   Had spoiled his nice new rattle.
>
> Just then flew down a monstrous crow,
>   As black as a tar-barrel;
> Which frightened both the heroes so,
>   They quite forgot their quarrel.

DUM

I know what you're thinking about; but it isn't so, nohow.

DEE

Contrariwise, if it was so, it might, and if it were so, it would be; but as it isn't, it ain't. That's logic.

ALICE

I was thinking which is the best way out of this wood: it's getting dark. Would you tell me, please?

Dum and Dee grin at each other.

ALICE
First Boy!

DUM
Nohow!

ALICE
Next Boy!

DEE [*Shouts*]
Contrariwise!

DUM
You've begun wrong. The first thing in a visit is to say
'How d'ye do' and shake hands! [*As they shake hands,
they dance in a ring and sing*: 'Here We Go Round the
Mulberry Bush.' *Suddenly they leave off dancing*]

ALICE [*Aside*]
It would never do to say 'How d'ye do?' *now*. We seem to
have got beyond that, somehow! [*To them*] I hope
you're not much tired?

DUM
Nohow. And thank you *very* much for asking.

DEE
So *much* obliged. You like poetry?

ALICE
Ye-es, pretty well – some poetry. Would you tell me which
road leads out of the wood?

DEE
What shall I repeat to her? [*Begin this at 'you' in Alice's
previous speech*]

DUM [*Hugging his brother*]
The 'Walrus and the Carpenter' is the longest.

DEE
The sun was shining –

ALICE
If it's very long, would you please tell me first which
road…

*Dum and Dee break in at 'you' in previous speech with
'The Walrus and the Carpenter'. They say all material not
in 'quotes'; the rest is spoken by members of Chorus.*

DEE
    The sun was shining on the sea,
      Shining with all his might:
    He did his very best to make
      The billows smooth and bright –
    And this was odd, because it was
      The middle of the night.

BARBER SHOP QUARTET
    'O and this was odd
      because it was
    The middle of the night
      the night.'

DUM
    The moon was shining sulkily,
      Because she thought the sun
    Had got no business to be there
      After the day was done –

MOON
    'It's very rude of him,'

DEE
> – she said,

MOON
'To come and spoil the fun!'

DEE
The sea was wet as wet could be,
The sands were dry as dry.
You could not see a cloud, because
No cloud was in the sky:
No birds were flying overhead –
There were no birds to fly.

DUM
The Walrus and the Carpenter
Were walking close at hand:
They wept like anything to see
Such quantities of sand:

CARPENTER AND WALRUS
'If this were only cleared away,'

DUM
> – They said,

CARPENTER AND WALRUS
'It would be grand!'

CARPENTER
'If seven maids with seven mops
Swept it for half a year,
Do you suppose,'

DEE
> – the Walrus said,

WALRUS
   'That they could get it clear?'

CARPENTER
   'I doubt it,'

DEE
                     – said the Carpenter,
   And shed a bitter tear.

WALRUS
   'O Oysters, come and walk with us!'

DUM
   The Walrus did beseech.

WALRUS
   'A pleasant walk, a pleasant talk,
      Along the briny beach:
   We cannot do with more than four,
      To give a hand to each.'

DEE
   The eldest Oyster looked at him,
      But never a word he said:
   The eldest Oyster winked his eye,
      And shook his heavy head –
   Meaning to say he did not choose
      To leave the oyster-bed.

DUM
   But four young Oysters hurried up,
      All eager for the treat:
   Their coats were brushed, their faces washed,
      Their shoes were clean and neat –
   And this was odd, because, you know,
      They hadn't any feet.

CARPENTER   Oysters to the Killing Fields   WALRUS

DEE
    Four other Oysters followed them,
      And yet another four;
   And thick and fast they came at last,
    And more, and more, and more –
   All hopping through the frothy waves,
     And scrambling to the shore.

DUM
    The Walrus and the Carpenter
     Walked on a mile or so,
   And then they rested on a rock
     Conveniently low:
   And all the little Oysters stood
     And waited in a row.

WALRUS
'The time has come,'

DEE
           – the Walrus said,

WALRUS
  'To talk of many things:
  Of shoes – and ships – and sealing wax –
  Of cabbages – and kings –
  And why the sea is boiling hot –
  And whether pigs have wings.'

OYSTERS
  'But wait a bit,'

DUM
                – the Oysters cried,

OYSTERS
  'Before we have our chat;
  For some of us are out of breath,
  And all of us are fat!'

CARPENTER
  'No hurry!'

DUM
                – said the Carpenter.
  They thanked him much for that.

WALRUS
  'A loaf of bread,'

DEE
                – the Walrus said,

WALRUS
  'Is what we chiefly need:
  Pepper and vinegar besides
  Are very good indeed –
  Now, if you're ready, Oysters dear,
  We can begin to feed.'

Carpenter (with bad cold), Selected Oysters & Walrus

OYSTERS
   'But not on us!'

DUM
                    – the Oysters cried,
   Turning a little blue.

OYSTERS
   'After such kindness, that would be
     A dismal thing to do!'

WALRUS
   'The night is fine,'

DUM
                    – the Walrus said,

WALRUS
   'Do you admire the view?
   'It was so kind of you to come!
     And you are very nice!'

DEE
The Carpenter said nothing but

CARPENTER
'Cut us another slice.
I wish you were not quite so deaf –
I've had to ask you twice!'

WALRUS
'It seems a shame,'

DUM
                    – the Walrus said,

WALRUS
'To play them such a trick.
After we've brought them out so far,
And made them trot so quick!'

DUM
The Carpenter said nothing but

CARPENTER
'The butter's spread too thick!'

WALRUS
'I weep for you,'

DUM
                    – the Walrus said:
'I deeply sympathize.'

DUM
With sobs and tears he sorted out
Those of the largest size,
Holding his pocket-handkerchief
Before his streaming eyes.

CARPENTER
    'O Oysters,'

DEE
                        – said the Carpenter,

CARPENTER
    'You've had a pleasant run!
    Shall we be trotting home again?'

DEE
    But answer came there none –
    And this was scarcely odd, because
    They'd eaten every one.

As the stage is cleared, we should now see revealed – the Red King.

ALICE   [*Pause as stage rearranged*]
I like the Walrus best because he was a *little* sorry for the poor oysters.

DEE
He ate more than the Carpenter, though. You see he held his handkerchief in front, so that the Carpenter couldn't count how many he took: contrariwise.

ALICE
That was mean! Then I like the Carpenter best – if he didn't eat so many as the Walrus.

DUM
But he ate as many as he could get!

ALICE
Well! They were both very unpleasant characters. [*Steam-engine puffings*] Are there any lions or tigers about here?

DEE
It's only the Red King snoring.

DEE AND DUM
Come and look at him! [*They take her hands*]

DUM
Isn't he a lovely sight?

DEE
Fit to snore his head off.

ALICE
I'm afraid he'll catch cold with lying on the damp grass.

DEE
He's dreaming now, and what do you think he's dreaming about?

ALICE
Nobody can guess that.

DEE
Why, about you! [*Pause*]   And if he left off dreaming about you, where do you suppose you'd be?

ALICE
Where I am now, of course.

DEE
Not you! You'd be nowhere. Why, you're only a sort of thing in his dream!

DUM
If that there King was to wake, you'd go out – bang! – just like a candle!

ALICE
I shouldn't. Besides, if *I'm* only a sort of thing in his dream, what are *you*, I should like to know.

DUM
Ditto.

DEE
Ditto, ditto!

ALICE
Hush, you'll be waking him, I'm afraid, if you make so much noise.

DUM
Well, it's no use *your* talking about waking him when you're only one of the things in his dream. You know very well you're not real.

ALICE
I *am* real!

DEE
You won't make yourself a bit realer by crying. There's nothing to cry about.

ALICE
If I wasn't real – I shouldn't be able to cry.

DUM
I hope you don't suppose those are *real* tears?

ALICE [*Aside*]
I know they're talking nonsense, and it's foolish to cry about it. [*Pause, brushing away tears*] At any rate, I'd better be getting out of the wood, for really it's coming on very dark. Do you think it's going to rain?

DEE [*Spreading the umbrella on ground behind them*]
No, I don't think it is. At least – not under here. Nohow.

ALICE
But it may rain *outside*?

DEE
It may – if it chooses. We've no objection. Contrariwise.

ALICE [*Aside*]
Selfish things! Goodnight!

DUM
Do you see that!

ALICE
It's only a rattle. Not a rattle-snake, you know. Only an old rattle – quite old and broken.

DUM
I knew it was. It's spoilt, of course!

ALICE
You needn't be so angry about an old rattle.

DUM
But it *isn't* old! It's *new*, I tell you – I bought it yesterday – my nice *new rattle*!

Tweedledee is trying to fold up the umbrella with himself in it but not quite succeeding. He rolls over, bundled up in umbrella, with only his head out. He opens and shuts his mouth, and then does the same with large eyes.

DUM
Of course you agree to have a battle?

DEE

I suppose so, only *she* must help us to dress up, you know.

Exits, returning with armour composed of bolsters, blankets, coal-scuttles etc.

DUM

I hope you're a good hand at pinning and tying strings? Everyone of these things has got to go on, somehow or other.

ALICE [*Dresses Dee first, aside*]

Really, they'll be more like bundles of old clothes than anything else, by the time they're ready! [*Holding up a bolster*]

DEE

To keep my head from being cut off! Stupid! [*Gravely*] You know it's one of the most serious things that can possibly happen to one in a battle – to get one's head cut off.

DUM

Do I look very pale?

ALICE

Well – yes – a *little*.

DUM [*Sotto voce*]

I'm very brave, generally, only to-day I happen to have a headache.

DEE

And *I've* got a toothache! I'm far worse than you!

ALICE

Then you'd better not fight to-day.

DUM

We *must* have a bit of a fight, but I don't care about going on long. What's the time now?

DEE

Half-past four.

DUM

Let's fight till six, and then have dinner.

DEE

Very well, and *she* can watch us – only you'd better not come *very* close. I generally hit everything I can see – when I get really excited.

DUM

And I hit everything within reach, whether I can see it or not!

ALICE [*Laughing*]

You must hit the trees pretty often, I should think.

DUM [*Looking around, smiling*]

I don't suppose, there'll be a tree left standing, for ever so far round, by the time we've finished.

ALICE

And all about a rattle!

DUM

I shouldn't have minded so much, if it hadn't been new.

ALICE [*Aside*]

I wish the monstrous crow would come!

DUM

There's only one sword, you know. But you can have the

umbrella – it's quite as sharp. Quick. It's getting as dark as it can.

DEE
And darker.

ALICE
What a thick, black cloud that is. I believe it's got wings.

Sounds of approaching hurricane. Some caws too.

DUM
It's the crow!   [*They both run off*]

ALICE   [*Taking shelter under a tree*]
It can't get me here! It's far too large to squeeze itself in among the trees, but I wish it wouldn't flap its wings so. [*Stage darkens. A white woollen shawl sweeps across the wood*]   Here's somebody's shawl being blown away!

   She nimbly fetches it down, and with difficulty holds onto it.

8. The White Queen

STUNT MAN VINCE AS WHITE QUEEN

In order to milk the visual fun of the Queen's running so, I wonder if it's possible to do some trick work here. Ray Bolger in Where's Charley *had a special slide installed on stage, I think it may have been greased black marble (greased with graphite?) upon which he could whiz. We need (stunt man?) a glimpse of the White Queen just rocketing through with maybe a mid-air somersault, and then a final run, more slowly, which brings her to Alice.*

ALICE
I'm very glad I happened to be in the way.
[*Helps Queen on with shawl*]

WHITE QUEEN
Bread and butter, bread and butter.

ALICE
Am I addressing the White Queen?

Stage begins to lighten somewhat....

WHITE QUEEN
Well, yes, if you call that a-dressing. It isn't my notion of the thing at all.

ALICE
If Your Majesty will only tell me the right way to begin,
I'll do it as well as I can.

WHITE QUEEN
But I don't want it done at all! I've been a-dressing myself
for the last two hours.

ALICE
May I put your shawl straight for you?

WHITE QUEEN
I don't know what's the matter with it! It's out of temper, I
think. I've pinned it here, and I've pinned it there, but
there's no pleasing it!

ALICE
Your shawl *can't* go straight, you know if you pin it all on
one side, and, dear me, what a state your hair is in!

WHITE QUEEN
The brush has got entangled in it! And I lost the comb yesterday.

ALICE [*Rights this situation and rearranges the Queen's
coiffure*]
Come, you look rather better now. But really you should
have a lady's maid!

WHITE QUEEN
I'm sure I'll take you with pleasure! Twopence a week and
jam every other day.

ALICE [*Laughing*]
I don't want you to hire *me* –
and I don't care for jam.

WHITE QUEEN
It's very good jam.

ALICE
Well, I don't want any *today*, at any rate.

WHITE QUEEN
You couldn't have it if you *did* want it. The rule is, jam tomorrow and jam yesterday – but never jam *today*.

ALICE
It must come sometimes to 'jam today.'

WHITE QUEEN
No, it can't. It's jam every *other* day: today isn't any *other* day, you know.

ALICE
I don't understand you. It's dreadfully confusing.

WHITE QUEEN
That's the effect of living backwards: it always makes me a little giddy at first –

ALICE
Living backwards! I never heard of such a thing!

WHITE QUEEN
But there's one great advantage in it, that one's memory works both ways.

ALICE
I'm sure *mine* only works one way. I can't remember things before they happen.

WHITE QUEEN
It's a poor sort of memory that only works backwards.

ALICE
What sort of things do you remember best?

WHITE QUEEN
Oh, things that happened the week after next. For instance, now, there's the King's Messenger. He's in prison now, being punished and the trial doesn't even begin till next Wednesday: and of course the crime comes last of all.

ALICE
Suppose he never commits the crime?

WHITE QUEEN
That would be all the better, wouldn't it? By the by, help me put this sticking plaster on my finger, will you like a helpful girl. All the better if he didn't commit the crime.

ALICE
Of course it would be all the better, but it wouldn't be all the better his being punished.

WHITE QUEEN
You're wrong *there*, at any rate. Were *you* ever punished?

ALICE
Only for faults.

WHITE QUEEN
And you were all the better for it. I know!

ALICE
Yes, but then I *had* done the things I was punished for. That makes all the difference.

WHITE QUEEN
But if you *hadn't* done them, that would have been better still; better, and better, and better –

ALICE
There's a mistake somewhere –

WHITE QUEEN
Oh, oh, oh! My finger's bleeding. Oh, oh, oh!

ALICE
What is the matter? Have you pricked your finger?

WHITE QUEEN
Not yet, but I soon shall – oh, oh, ... oh!

ALICE
When do you expect to do it?

WHITE QUEEN
When I fasten my shawl again, the brooch will come
undone, directly. Oh, oh! The brooch is flying open.

ALICE
Take care! You're holding the brooch all crooked. The pin
has slipped, and Your Majesty has pricked her finger!!!

WHITE QUEEN [Serenely]
That accounts for the bleeding, you see. Now you understand the way things happen around here.

ALICE
Why don't you scream now?

WHITE QUEEN
Why, I've done all the screaming already. What would be
the good of having it all over again?

ALICE
The crow must have flown away, I think. I'm so glad it's
gone. I thought it was the night coming on.

WHITE QUEEN
I wish I could manage to be glad! Only I never can remember the rule. You must be very happy, living in this wood, and being glad whenever you like!

ALICE [*Crying*]
Only it is so *very* lonely here.

WHITE QUEEN
Oh, don't go on like that! [*Wringing her hands*] Consider what a great girl you are. Consider what a long way you've come today. Consider what o'clock it is. Consider anything, only don't cry!

ALICE [*Laughing*]
Can you keep from crying by considering things?

WHITE QUEEN
That's the way it is done.
Nobody can do two things at once.
How old are you?

ALICE
I'm eleven and a half, exactly.

WHITE QUEEN
You needn't say 'exactly.' I can believe it without that. Now – ! I'll give you something to believe. I'm just one hundred and one, five months and a day old.

ALICE
I can't believe *that*!

WHITE QUEEN
Can't you? Try again: draw a long breath, and shut your eyes.

ALICE [*Laughing*]
There's no use trying, one *can't* believe impossible things.

WHITE QUEEN
I daresay you haven't had much practice. When I was your age, I always did it for half an hour a day. Why sometimes I've believed as many as six impossible things before breakfast. [*Wind blows*] There goes the shawl again. [*Brook sound*] Now you shall see me pin it on again, all by myself!

ALICE
Then I hope your finger is better now?

Brook sounds very loud, then the White Queen begins to change into a knitting sheep; perhaps the shawl opens out into the appropriate shape.

9. The Sheep in the Shop

WHITE QUEEN
Oh, much better! Much be-etter! Be-etter! Be-etter! Be-e-ehh! Bah! Maaah!

ALICE
Am I really in a shop? And has she turned into a sheep?

SHEEP
What is it you want to buy?

ALICE [*Apprehensively*]
I don't *quite* know yet. I should like to look all round me first, if I might.

SHEEP
You may look in front of you, and on both sides, if you like, but you can't look *all* round you – unless you've got eyes at the back of your head.

When Alice reaches for a doll or a work-box or a toy Jabberwock, some invisible hand shifts it to a higher shelf or leads her in a circle.

ALICE
Things flow about so here!

She tries to catch the toy by smacking her hands down on higher and higher shelves, in more circular movements.

ALICE
Sometimes it's a doll and then it changes into a workbox and then it changes into... [*Pursued toy becomes Jabberwock's head and then...*]

SHEEP
Jabberwocky!

NARRATOR
   'Twas brillig, and the slithy toves
     Did gyre and gimble in the wabe:
   All mimsy were the borogoves,
     And the mome raths outgrabe.

FATHER
   'Beware the Jabberwock, my son!
     The jaws that bite, the claws that catch!
   Beware the Jubjub bird, and shun
     The frumious Bandersnatch!'

   NARRATOR
     He took his vorpal sword in hand:

"Beware the frumious bandersnatch?"
Father and Son (Jabberwocky)

Long time the manxome foe he sought –
So rested he by the Tumtum tree,
And stood awhile in thought.

And, as in uffish thought he stood,
  The Jabberwock, with eyes of flame,
Came whiffling through the tulgey wood,
  And burbled as it came!

One, two! One, two! And through and through
  The vorpal blade went snicker-snack!
He left it dead, and with its head
  He went galumphing back.

FATHER
  'And hast thou slain the Jabberwock?
    Come to my arms, my beamish boy!
  O frabjous day! Callooh! Callay!'
    He chortled in his joy.

Jabberwock disappears.

NARRATOR
  'Twas brillig, and the slithy toves
    Did gyre and gimble in the wabe:
  All mimsy were the borogoves,
    And the mome raths outgrabe.

SHEEP
Now, what *do* you want to buy?

ALICE
Well, not a Jabberwock! To buy. [*Pause*] I should like to
buy an egg, please. How do you sell them?

NARRATOR
Fivepence farthing for one. Twopence for two.

ALICE
Then two are cheaper than one?

NARRATOR
Only you *must* eat them both, if you buy two.

ALICE
Then I'll have *one*, please.   [*Aside*]   They mightn't be at
all nice, you know.

NARRATOR   [*Taking money*]
I never put things into people's hands – that would never
do – you must get it for yourself.

*Taking the egg which is already puffing up like a white
balloon to the other end of the shop, she sets it up on a
shelf which is really the wall that Humpty Dumpty
stands or sits on.*

ALICE
I wonder *why* it wouldn't do?   [*Groping in the dark*]   The
egg seems to get further away the more I walk towards it.
How very odd to find trees growing here! And actually
here's a little brook! Well, this is the very queerest shop I
ever saw! Little brook – that means I'm come, I have come
to – Square Six!   [*The egg gets larger and larger until she
sees clearly that it is Humpty Dumpty!*]   It can't be anybody else but Humpty Dumpty. And how exactly like an
egg he is!

End of ACT ONE

Act Two

Alice Through the Looking glass: Stratford Festival 94

Humpty Dumpty

10. Humpty Dumpty

The curtain flies open revealing Humpty Dumpty sitting on a very narrow high wall, legs crossed, staring ahead without noticing Alice. From time to time he shakes with an ominous tumbly sound, then recovers, making us nervous.

HUMPTY [*Looking away from her*]
It's *very* provoking to be called an egg – *very*!

ALICE
I said you *looked* like an egg, Sir. And some eggs are very pretty, you know.

HUMPTY [*Still looking away*]
Some people have no more sense than a baby.

ALICE
　　Humpty Dumpty sat on a wall:
　　Humpty Dumpty had a great fall.
　　All the King's horses and all the King's men
　　Couldn't put Humpty Dumpty in his place again.

That last line is much too long for the poetry, isn't it?

HUMPTY
Don't stand chattering to yourself like that, but tell me your name and your business.

ALICE
Well, my *name* is Alice, but –

HUMPTY
It's a stupid name enough! What does it mean?

ALICE
Must a name mean something?

HUMPTY
Of course it must. [*Short laugh*]
My name means the shape I am – and a good handsome shape it is, too. With a name like yours, you might be any shape, almost.

ALICE
Why do you sit out here all alone?

HUMPTY
Why, because there's nobody with me! Did you think I didn't know the answer to *that*? Ask another.

ALICE
Don't you think you'd be safer down on the ground? That wall is so *very* narrow!

HUMPTY
What tremendously easy riddles you ask! [*Growling*]
Of course I don't think so! Why, if ever I *did* fall off – which there's no chance of – but *if* I did   [*Pursing his lips, grandly and solemnly*]   If I *did* fall, *the King has promised me* – ah, you may turn pale, if you like. You didn't think I was going to say that, did you? *The King has promised me – with his very own mouth –* to – to –

ALICE
To send all his horses and all his men.

HUMPTY
Now I declare that's too bad! You've been listening at doors – and behind trees – and down chimneys – or you couldn't have known it!

ALICE
I haven't, indeed! It's in a book.

HUMPTY
Ah, well! They may write such things in a *book*. That's what they call a History of England, that is. Now, take a good look at me. I'm one that has spoken to a King, *I* am: mayhap you'll never see such another: and, to show you I'm not proud, you may shake hands with me!

They shake hands.

HUMPTY
Yes, all his horses and all his men. They'd pick me up again in a minute, *they* would! However, this conversation is going on a little too fast: let's go back to the last remark but one.

ALICE
I'm afraid I can't quite remember it.

HUMPTY
In that case we may start afresh, and it's my turn to choose a subject –

ALICE [*Aside*]
He talks about it just as if it was a game! [*Suddenly*] What a beautiful belt you've got on! [*As suddenly seeing that it may be something else*] At least, a beautiful cravat, I should have said – no, a belt, I mean – I beg your pardon! [*Aside*] If only I knew which was neck and which was waist.

HUMPTY [*Growling, after a pause*]
It is a – *most* – *provoking* – thing when a person doesn't know a cravat from a belt!

ALICE
I know it's very ignorant of me.

HUMPTY
It's a cravat, child, and a beautiful one, as you say. It's a present from the White King and Queen. There now!

ALICE
Is it really?

HUMPTY
They gave it me … [*Crossing knees the other way and very nearly falling off*] They gave it me – for an un-birthday present.

ALICE
I beg your pardon?

HUMPTY
I'm not offended.

ALICE
I mean, what *is* an un-birthday present?

HUMPTY
A present given when it isn't your birthday, of course.

ALICE
Then – I like birthday presents best.

HUMPTY
You don't know what you're talking about! How many days are there in a year?

ALICE
Three hundred and sixty-five.

HUMPTY
And how many birthdays have you?

ALICE
One.

HUMPTY
And if you take one from three hundred and sixty-five, what remains?

ALICE
Three hundred and sixty-four of course.

HUMPTY
Therefore there are three hundred and sixty-four days when you might get un-birthday presents –

ALICE
Certainly.

HUMPTY
And only *one* for birthday presents, you know. There's glory for you!

ALICE
I don't know what you mean by 'glory'.

HUMPTY [*Contemptuous smile*]
Of course you don't – till I tell you. I meant 'There's a nice knock-down argument for you!'

ALICE
But 'glory' doesn't mean 'a nice knock-down argument'.

HUMPTY
When *I* use a word, it means just what I choose it to mean – neither more nor less.

ALICE
The question is whether you *can* make words mean so many different things.

HUMPTY
The question is, which is to be master – that's all. [*Pause as Alice ponders this*] They've a temper, some of them – particularly verbs. They're the proudest – adjectives you can do anything with, but not verbs – however, *I* can manage the whole lot of them! Impenetrability! That's what *I* say!

ALICE
Would you tell me, please, what that means?

HUMPTY
Now you talk like a reasonable child. I meant by 'impenetrability' that we've had enough of that subject, and it would be just as well if you'd mention what you mean to do next, as I suppose you don't mean to stop here all the rest of your life.

ALICE
That's a great deal to make one word mean.

HUMPTY
When I make a word do a lot of work like that, I always pay it extra.

ALICE
Oh!

HUMPTY
Ah, you should see 'em come round me of a Saturday night for to get their wages, you know.

ALICE
You seem very clever at explaining words, Sir. Would you

kindly tell me the meaning of the poem called 'Jabberwocky'?

HUMPTY
Let's hear it. I can explain all the poems that ever were
invented – and a good many that haven't been invented
just yet.

ALICE
    'Twas brillig, and the slithy toves
    Did gyre and gimble in the wabe:
    All mimsy were the borogoves,
    And the mome raths outgrabe.

HUMPTY
That's enough to begin with: there are plenty of hard
words there. 'Brillig.' 'Brillig' means four o'clock in the
afternoon – the time when you begin broiling things for
dinner.

ALICE
That'll do very well, and 'slithy'?

HUMPTY
Well, 'slithy' means 'lithe and slimy'. 'Lithe' is the same
as 'active'. You see it's like a portmanteau – there are two
meanings packed up into one word.

ALICE
I see it now, and what are 'toves'?

HUMPTY
Well, 'toves' are something like badgers – they're something like lizards – and they're something like corkscrews.

ALICE
They must be very curious-looking creatures.

HUMPTY
They are that: also they make their nests under sun-dials –
also they live on cheese.

ALICE
And what's to 'gyre' and to 'gimble'?

HUMPTY
To 'gyre' is to go round and round like a gyroscope. To
'gimble' is to make holes like a gimblet.

ALICE
And 'the wabe' is the grass-plot round a sun-dial, I suppose?

HUMPTY
Of course it is. It's called 'wabe,' you know, because it
goes a long way before it, and a long way behind it –

ALICE
And a long way beyond it on each side.

HUMPTY
Exactly so. Well then, 'mimsy' is 'flimsy and miserable'
(there's another portmanteau for you). And a 'borogove' is
a thin shabby-looking bird with its feathers sticking out
all round – something like a live mop.

ALICE
And then 'mome raths'? I'm afraid I'm giving you a great
deal of trouble.

HUMPTY
Well, a 'rath' is a sort of green pig: but 'mome' I'm not certain about. I think it's short for 'from home' – meaning
that they'd lost their way, you know.

ALICE
And what does 'outgrabe' mean?

HUMPTY
Well, 'outgribing' is something between bellowing and whistling, with a kind of sneeze in the middle: however, you'll hear it done, maybe – down in the wood yonder – and, when you've once heard it, you'll be *quite* content. Who's been repeating all this hard stuff to you?

ALICE
I read it in a book.
But I *had* some poetry repeated to me, much easier than that, by – Tweedledee I think it was.

HUMPTY
As to poetry, you know, I can repeat poetry as well as other folk, if it comes to that –

ALICE [*Worried*]
Oh, it needn't come to that!

HUMPTY
The piece I'm going to repeat was written entirely for your amusement.

ALICE [*Sadly*]
Thank you.

HUMPTY
   In winter, when the fields are white,
   I sing this song for your delight
only I don't sing it.

ALICE
I see you don't.

HUMPTY
If you can *see* whether I'm singing or not, you've sharper
eyes than most.
    In spring, when woods are getting green,
    I'll try and tell you what I mean.

ALICE
Thank you very much.

HUMPTY
    In summer, when the days are long,
    Perhaps you'll understand the song.

    In autumn, when the leaves are brown,
    Take pen and ink and write it down.

ALICE
I will if I can remember it so long.

HUMPTY
You needn't go on making remarks like that; they're not
sensible, and they put me out.
    I sent a message to the fish
    I told them 'This is what I wish.'

    The little fishes' answer was
    'We cannot do it, Sir, because –

ALICE
I'm afraid I don't quite understand.

HUMPTY
It gets easier further on.
    I took a kettle large and new,
    Fit for the deed I had to do.

My heart went hop, my heart went thump:
I filled the kettle at the pump.

Then some one came to me and said:

Enter a member of cast as messenger.

MESSENGER
  'The little fishes are in bed.'

HUMPTY
  I said to him, I said it plain.
  'Then you must wake them up again.'

  I said it very loud and clear:
  I went and shouted in his ear!
  [*With voice rising to a scream*]
  'Then you must wake them up again'

ALICE
I wouldn't have been the messenger for *anything*!

HUMPTY
  But he was very stiff and proud:
  He said:

MESSENGER
  'You needn't shout so loud!'

HUMPTY
  And he was very proud and stiff:
  He said:

MESSENGER
  'I'd go and wake them, if – '

HUMPTY

I took a corkscrew from the shelf:
I went to wake them up myself.

And when I found the door was locked,
I pulled and pushed and kicked and knocked,

And when I found the door was shut,
I tried to turn the handle, but –

ALICE
Is that all?

HUMPTY
That's all. Goodbye.

ALICE
Goodbye, till we meet again.   [*Holds out her hand*]

HUMPTY   [*Gives her one of his fingers to shake*]
I shouldn't know you again if we *did* meet. You're so
exactly like other people.

ALICE
The face is what one goes by, generally.

HUMPTY
That's just what I complain of. Your face is the same as
everybody has – the two eyes,   [*Thumbs mark eye-places*]
nose in the middle, mouth under. It's always the same.
Now if you had the two eyes on the same side of the nose,
for instance – or the mouth at the top – that would be
some help.

ALICE
It wouldn't look nice.

HUMPTY
Wait till you've tried.   [*Glides out of sight*]

ALICE
Goodbye!   [*As she walks away*]   Of all the unsatisfactory
– of all the unsatisfactory people I *ever* met –

*A heavy crash shakes the forest from end to end. Soldiers
come running in a throng that soars from ten pairs to
thousands! – filling the whole woods. Alice hides behind
a tree.*

This is the biggest production scene in Looking-Glass
*and Carroll has hired hundreds of extras; in essence, the
entire cast sieve through the forest scene – with heavy
support by sound for their horses stumbling, the soldiers
tripping, others falling on top of them, climaxing in heaps
of men, little heaps. As these roll off stage in the direction
of the crash sound, Alice comes upon the White King, sitting on the ground writing in his memorandum book.*

11. All the King's Men: The Lion and the Unicorn

WHITE KING
All the King's soldiers, all the King's men – I've sent them all! Did you happen to meet any soldiers, my dear, as you came through the wood?

ALICE
Yes, I did. Several thousand, I should think.

WHITE KING
Four thousand two hundred and seven, that's the exact number. [*Checking his book*] I couldn't send *all* the horses, because two of them are wanted in the game. And I haven't sent the Two Messengers, either. They're both

Alice: "What curious attitudes he goes into!"

White King: Not at all. He's an Anglo-Saxon Messenger —and those are Anglo-Saxon attitudes

gone to the town. Just look along the road, and tell me if you can see either of them.

ALICE
I see nobody on the road.

WHITE KING
I only wish *I* had such eyes. To be able to see Nobody! And at that distance too! Why, it's as much as *I* can do to see real people, by this light!

ALICE
I see somebody now! But he's coming very slowly – and what curious attitudes he goes into!

WHITE KING
Not at all. He's an Anglo-Saxon Messenger – and those are Anglo-Saxon attitudes. He only does them when he's happy. His name is Haigha. [*Pronounced Hayor to rhyme with Mayor*]

ALICE
I love my love with an H because he is Happy. I hate him with an H because he is Hideous. I fed him with – with – with – with Ham-sandwiches and Hay. His name is Haigha, and he lives –

WHITE KING
He lives on the Hill. The other messenger's called Hatta. I must have *two*, you know – to come and go. One to come, and one to go.

ALICE
I beg your pardon?

WHITE KING
It isn't respectable to beg.

ALICE

I only meant that I didn't understand. Why one to come and one to go?

WHITE KING

Didn't I tell you? I must have *two* – to fetch and carry. One to fetch, and one to carry.

The March Hare Messenger arrives tired, waving his hands, eyes rolling, writhing in the attitudes figures take in Anglo-Saxon manuscripts – the effect of calligraphers completely triumphing over our anatomy.

WHITE KING

You alarm me! I feel faint. Give me a ham sandwich!

Messenger opens his bag and proffers same.

WHITE KING   [*After bolting this*]
Another sandwich!

HARE   [*Peeping into bag*]
There's nothing but hay left now.

WHITE KING

Hay, then.   [*Faint whisper*]   There's nothing like hay, eating hay when you're faint.   [*Munching*]

ALICE

I should think throwing cold water over you would be better.

WHITE KING

I didn't say there was nothing better. I said there was nothing *like* it.   [*Pause, as Alice does not deny this*]   Who did you pass on the road?

HARE
Nobody.

WHITE KING
Quite right. The young lady saw him too. So of course
Nobody walks slower than you. [*Prototype for the
'Who's on First?' vaudeville routine beloved by Abbot
and Costello*]

HARE
I do my best.
I'm sure nobody walks much faster than I do.

WHITE KING
He can't do that, or else he'd have been here first. However, now you've got your breath, you may tell us what's
happened in the town.

HARE
I'll whisper it. [*Cupping his hands, stooping by King's
ear then shouts*] They're at it again!

WHITE KING [*Jumps up*]
Do you call *that* a whisper? If you do such a thing again,
I'll have you buttered! It went through and through my
head like an earthquake!

ALICE
It would have to be a very tiny earthquake. Who are at it
again?

WHITE KING
They, the Lion and the Unicorn, of course.

ALICE
Fighting for the crown?

WHITE KING

Yes, to be sure, and the best of the joke is, that it's *my* crown all the while! Let's run and see them.

Staged as with Red Queen's running.

ALICE

The Lion and the Unicorn were fighting for the crown:
The Lion beat the Unicorn all round the town.
Some gave them white bread, some gave them brown:
Some gave them plum-cake and drummed them out of town.
[*Panting*] Does – the one – that wins – get the crown?

WHITE KING

Dear me, no! What an idea!

ALICE

Would you – be good enough [*Panting*] to stop a minute – just to get – one's breath again? [*Perhaps they run on the treadmill used for the Red Queen's famous gallop*]

WHITE KING

I'm *good* enough, only I'm not *strong* enough. You see, a minute goes by so fearfully quick. You might as well try to stop a Bandersnatch!

Already we have heard the crowd cheering on the fighters at a distance. Now they enter with a boxing ring on casters rolled on. In boxing trunks, the Lion and Unicorn are boxing. Hatta (Mad Hatter) is watching the fight with teacup and bread piece at hand. So is the whole cast.

He's only just out of prison. [*Referring to other messenger*] And he hadn't finished his tea when he was sent in, and they only give them oyster-shells in there – so you see he's very hungry and thirsty. How are you dear child? [*Puts arm around Hatta who nods, goes on munching*]

HARE
Were you happy in prison, dear child?

Hatta looks around, says nothing, starts to cry.

HARE
Speak, can't you –

WHITE KING
Speak, won't you!
How are they getting on with the fight?

HATTA   [*Swallowing, then in choked tones*]
They're getting on very well.   [*Tries to clear throat*]
Each of them has been down about eighty-seven times.

ALICE
Then I suppose they'll soon bring the white bread and the
brown?

HATTA
It's waiting for 'em now; this is a bit of it as I'm eating.

WHITE KING
Ten minutes for refreshments!

*Haigha and Hatta carry round trays of white and brown
bread. Alice tries some, but as in the case of the Red
Queen's biscuit, Looking-glass bread is very, very dry.*

WHITE KING
I don't think they'll fight any more today.   [*To Hatta*]   Go
and order the drums to begin.

*The Hatter bounds off like a grasshopper. Alice looks
after him, then...*

ALICE
Look, look! There's the White Queen running across the country! She came flying out of the wood over yonder – How fast those Queens can run!

WHITE KING
There's some enemy after her, no doubt. That wood's full of them.

We see Red Knight in pursuit.

ALICE
But aren't you going to run and help her?

WHITE KING
My dear, I can only move one square at a time. No use, no use! She runs so fearfully quick. You might as well try to catch a Bandersnatch! But I'll make a memorandum about her, if you like. She's a dear good creature. [*Opens book*] Do you spell 'creature' with a double 'e'?

UNICORN [*Saunters by*]
I had the best of it this time.

WHITE KING [*Nervously*]
A little, a little. You shouldn't have run him through with your horn, you know.

UNICORN [*Carelessly*]
I didn't hurt him.
[*Catches sight of Alice, turns round, and looks at her with disgust*] What – is – this?

HAIGHA (HARE)
This is a child! We only found it today. It's as large as life, and twice as natural!

UNICORN
I always thought they were fabulous monsters! Is it alive?

HAIGHA
It can talk.

UNICORN
Talk, child.

ALICE
Do you know, I always thought Unicorns were fabulous monsters, too? I never saw one alive before!

UNICORN
Well, now that we *have* seen each other, if you'll believe in me, I'll believe in you. Is that a bargain?

ALICE
Yes, if you like.

UNICORN
Come, fetch out the plum-cake, old man!
  [*Turning to the King*]   None of your brown bread for me!

WHITE KING   [*To Haigha*]
Open the bag! Quick! Not that one – that's full of hay!

Haigha takes out a large plum-cake which he gives to Alice, then also produces a dish and a carving-knife. Sleepy Lion joins them.

LION   [*Deep hollow voice like Big Ben.*]
What's this!

UNICORN
Ah, what *is* it, now? You'll never guess! *I* couldn't.

LION [*Wearily*]
Are you animal or [*Yawn*] vegetable [*Yawn*] or min-
eral? [*Yawning*]

UNICORN
It's a fabulous monster!

LION
Then hand round the plum-cake, Monster. And sit down,
both of you. Fair play with the cake, you know!

UNICORN [*Looking at King's crown*]
What a fight we might have for the crown, *now*!

King's head shakes nervously.

LION
I should win easy.

UNICORN
I'm not so sure of that.

LION [*Angrily*]
Why, I beat you all round the town, you chicken!

WHITE KING [*Interrupting*]
All round the town? That's a good long way. Did you go by
the old bridge, or the market-place? You get the best view
by the old bridge.

LION [*Growling*]
I'm sure I don't know. There was too much dust to see
anything. What a time the Monster is, cutting up that
cake!

*Brook sound, reminding us that Alice is sitting by one,
but also that Square Six is just about over.*

ALICE [*Sawing away at the cake with no success*]
It's very provoking! I've cut several slices already, but they always join on again.

UNICORN
You don't know how to manage Looking-glass cakes. Hand it round first, and cut it afterwards.

Alice carries the dish around, the plum-cake divides itself into three pieces; she is left with the empty dish.

LION
Now cut it up.

Alice puzzles over dish and knife, cuts an invisible cake.

UNICORN
I say, this isn't fair! The Monster has given the Lion twice as much as me!

LION
She's kept none for herself, anyhow. Do you like plum-cake, Monster?

Drumming off stage, and then in a precision squad, the rest of the company cross the stage beating drums; they take the Lion and the Unicorn off with them. Alice holds her ears, springs across brook.

CHORUS
White Pawn to Queen 7.

ALICE [*With dish in hand*]
If that doesn't drum them out of town, nothing ever will.

12. Knights in the Forest

ALICE
So, I wasn't dreaming, after all, unless – unless we're all part of the same dream. Only I do hope it's my dream, and not the Red King's! I don't like belonging to another person's dream. I've a great mind to go and wake him, and see what happens!

RED KNIGHT [*Off stage*]
Ahoy! Ahoy! Check!

This Red Knight might be seen as being dressed in crimson armour galloping in on a 'horse' propelled by members of the company. He brandishes a big club and, dramatically, this is a terrifying attempt to prevent Alice from achieving her quest. Draw out his entry somewhat with the Knight's horse manoeuvring in the L-shaped move the piece does in chess, and charging apparently not in line with Alice, but at the last moment making the 90-degree angle turn.

RED KNIGHT
You're my prisoner!
[*Tumbles off horse, regains saddle*]
I hold your King and Queen in check, and I take you – Red to win! You'll never be a queen now. I take you–

WHITE KNIGHT [*Calls from off stage*]
Ahoy! Ahoy! Check!

With much the same sound and patterning as in the Red Knight's entry, tumbles off horse, gets up on saddle and the two Knights look at each other.

White Knight

RED KNIGHT
She's *my* prisoner, you know!

WHITE KNIGHT
Yes, but then *I* came and rescued her!

RED KNIGHT
Well, we must fight for her, then. [*Putting on helmet*]

WHITE KNIGHT [*Putting on helmet, then taking it off to say*] You will observe the Rules of Battle, of course?

RED KNIGHT
I always do.

Red and White Knight off stage with Alice watching. We hear banging blows, fury of insane combat. Alice hides behind tree.

ALICE [*Peeping out from behind tree with many withdrawals*] I wonder, now, what the Rules of Battle are. One Rule seems to be, that if one knight hits the other, he knocks him off his horse; and, if he misses, he tumbles off himself.

Onstage. They rise, shake hands, and Red Knight gallops off. The falls have ironmongery sounds.

Red Knight En **Passant**

WHITE KNIGHT [*Panting*]
It was a glorious victory, wasn't it?

ALICE
I don't know. I don't want to be anybody's prisoner. I want to be a Queen.

WHITE KNIGHT
So you will, when you've crossed the next brook. I'll see you safe to the end of the wood – and then I must go back, you know. That's the end of my move.   [*Trying to take off his helmet*]

ALICE
Thank you very much. May I help you off with your helmet?

WHITE KNIGHT
Now one can breathe more easily.

Alice looks at, for a start, a small box, fastened across his shoulders. As well, there are carrots tied to his saddle, a beehive, etc.

WHITE KNIGHT
I see you're admiring my little box. It's my own invention – to keep clothes and sandwiches in. You see I carry it upside down, so that the rain can't get in.

ALICE
But the things can get *out*. Do you know the lid's open?

WHITE KNIGHT
I didn't know it. Then all the things must have fallen out! And the box is no use without them.   [*He is about to toss the box away but after a pause he hangs it up on the tree*] Can you guess why I did that?   [*Alice shakes her head*]

In hopes some bees may make a nest in it – then I should get the honey.

ALICE
But you've got a bee-hive – or something like one – fastened to the saddle.

WHITE KNIGHT
Yes, it's a very good bee-hive, one of the best of its kind. But not a single bee has come near it yet. And the other thing is a mouse-trap. I suppose the mice keep the bees out – or the bees keep the mice out, I don't know which.

ALICE
I was wondering what the mouse-trap was for. It isn't very likely there would be any mice on the horse's back.

WHITE KNIGHT
Not very likely, perhaps, but, if they *do* come, I don't choose to have them running all about. [*Pause*] You see, it's as well to be provided for *everything*. That's the reason the horse has all those anklets round his feet.

ALICE
But what are they for?

WHITE KNIGHT
To guard against the bites of sharks. It's an invention of my own. And now help me on, I'll go with you to the end of the wood – What's that dish for?

ALICE
It's meant for plum-cake.

WHITE KNIGHT
We'd better take it with us. It'll come in handy if we find any plum-cake. Help me get it into this bag.

'The bag' can become a routine, Alice holding it open, the Knight proving the most awkward putter-of-things-into-bags conceivable.

WHITE KNIGHT
It's rather a tight fit, you see. There are so many candle-sticks in the bag. [*After this is accomplished*] I hope you've got your hair well fastened on?

ALICE
Only in the usual way.

WHITE KNIGHT
That's hardly enough. You see the wind is so *very* strong here. It's as strong as soup.

The Knight keeps falling off his horse: (a) when horse stops – falls in front, (b) when it goes on again – falls backwards, (c) falls sideways partly because the horse remembers all too well those L-shaped moves the knight makes in chess. Alice learns to walk clear of her side of the horse since it seems the favourite 'sideways' position for having a fall.

ALICE
I'm afraid you've not had much practice in riding.

WHITE KNIGHT [*Surprised and offended*]
What makes you say that? [*Scrambling back into saddle, using Alice's hair as a support*]

ALICE
Because people don't fall off quite so often, when they've had much practice.

WHITE KNIGHT [*Gravely*]
I've had plenty of practice. Plenty of practice.

ALICE
Indeed?

WHITE KNIGHT
The great art of riding is to keep –

Alice picks him up.

ALICE
I hope no bones are broken.

WHITE KNIGHT
None to speak of. The great art of riding, as I was saying is
– to keep your balance properly. Like this, you know –

*He lets go of bridle, stretches out both his arms, falls flat
on his back underneath the horse's feet.*

WHITE KNIGHT
Plenty of practice!   [*Keeps repeating as she gets him up
on his feet again*]   Plenty of practice!

ALICE
How *can* you go on talking so quietly, head downwards?
[*She drags him up and out, heaps him on the bank of the
ditch*]

WHITE KNIGHT
What does it matter where my body happens to be? My
mind goes on working all the same. In fact, the more head
downwards I am, the more I keep inventing new things.
Now the cleverest thing of the sort that I ever did ...
[*Pause*]   You are sad, let me sing you a song to comfort
you.

ALICE
Is it very long?

WHITE KNIGHT
It's long, but it's very, *very* beautiful. Everybody that hears me sing it – either it brings the *tears* into their eyes, or else – [*Sudden pause*]

ALICE
Or else what?

WHITE KNIGHT
Or else it doesn't, you know. The name of the song is called 'Haddocks' Eyes'.

ALICE
Oh, that's the name of the song, is it?

WHITE KNIGHT
No, you don't understand. That's what the name is *called*. The name really is 'The Aged Aged Man'.

ALICE
Then I ought to have said 'That's what the *song* is called?'

WHITE KNIGHT
No, you oughtn't; that's quite another thing! The *song* is called 'Ways and Means'; but that's only what it's *called*, you know!

ALICE
Well, what *is* the song, then?

WHITE KNIGHT
I was coming to that. The song really is 'A-sitting On a Gate' and the tune is my own invention.

The White Knight beats time to the tune which he whistles and hums.

WHITE KNIGHT
  I'll tell thee everything I can:
    There's little to relate.
  I saw an aged, aged man,
    A-sitting on a gate.

Old Man and Chorus enter with gate

WHITE KNIGHT
  'Who are you, aged man?' I said.
    'And how is it you live?'
  And his answer trickled through my head,
    Like water through a sieve.
  He said:

OLD MAN
  'I look for butterflies
    That sleep among the wheat:
  I make them into mutton-pies
    And sell them in the street.
  I sell them unto men,'

CHORUS
  – he said

OLD MAN
    'Who sail on stormy seas:
  And that's the way I get my bread –
    A trifle, if you please.'

WHITE KNIGHT
  But I was thinking of a plan
    To dye one's whiskers green,
  And always use so large a fan
    That they could not be seen.
  So, having no reply to give
    To what the old man said,

I cried,

    'Come, tell me how you live!'
And thumped him on the head.

    His accents mild took up the tale:
He said,

OLD MAN
    'I go my ways,
And when I find a mountain-rill,
    I set it in a blaze:
And thence they make a stuff they call
    Rowland's Macassar-Oil
Yet twopence-halfpenny is all
    They give me for my toil.

[*With resigned look*]

    I sometimes dig for buttered rolls,
        Or set limed twigs for crabs:
    I sometimes search the grassy knolls
        For wheels of Hansom-cabs.
    And that's the way'

CHORUS
    – (he gave a wink)

OLD MAN
    'By which I get my wealth –
And very gladly will I drink
    Your Honour's noble health.'

WHITE KNIGHT
    But I was thinking of a way
        To feed oneself on batter,

And so go on from day to day
   Getting a little fatter.
I shook him well from side to side,
   Until his face was blue:

CHORUS
   'Come tell me how you live,' I cried
     'And what it is you do!'
   He said,

WHITE KNIGHT AND CHORUS
   'And now, if e'er by chance I put
     My fingers into glue,
   Or madly squeeze a right-hand foot
     Into a left-hand shoe,
   Or if I drop upon my toe
     A very heavy weight,
   I weep, for it reminds me so
   Of that old man I used to know –
   Whose look was mild, whose speech was slow
   Whose hair was whiter than the snow,
   Whose face was very like a crow,
   With eyes, like cinders, all aglow,
   Who seemed distracted with his woe,
   Who rocked his body to and fro,
   And muttered mumblingly and low,
   As if his mouth were full of dough,
   Who snorted like a buffalo –
   That summer evening long ago,
   A-sitting on a gate.'

WHITE KNIGHT [*Takes up reins*]
You've only a few yards to go, down the hill and over that little brook, and then you'll be a Queen. But you'll stay and see me off first? I shan't be long. You'll wait and wave your handkerchief when I get to that turn in the road! I think it'll encourage me, you see.

ALICE

Of course I'll wait, and thank you very much for coming so far – and for the song – I liked it very much.

WHITE KNIGHT

I hope so. [*Doubtfully*] But you didn't cry so much as I thought you would.

They shake hands; he disappears.

ALICE

It won't take long to see him *off*, I expect. [*Sound*] There he goes! Right on his head as usual! However, he gets on again pretty easily – that comes of having so many things hung round the horse –

Goes on talking to herself, shaking her shoulders when she sees him take a tumble, finally waving her handkerchief. We don't see the tumbles. Since he's wearing tin armour, we hear them getting further away.

ALICE

I hope it encouraged him. And now for the last brook, and to be a Queen. How grand it sounds. [*Brook sound*] The Eighth Square at last!

She runs and jumps across the brook.

13. Coronation and Examination

After skipping about with joy, she lies down on the ground.

ALICE
Oh, how glad I am to get here! And what is this on my head? And how can it have got there without my knowing it? Well, this *is* grand! I never expected I should be a Queen so soon – and I'll tell you what it is, your Majesty, it'll never do for you to be lolling about on the grass like that! Queens have to be dignified, you know!

She gets up, walks about stiffly, crown almost comes off, then she gets the hang of it, walks over to brook to see what she looks like (sound of brook), crown falls in (splash), she retrieves it, regains confidence.

ALICE
Thank goodness, no one saw that, and if I really am a Queen I shall be able to manage it quite well in time.

There should be a moment of stillness reminding us of the time just before her first move. Suddenly Red Queen and White Queen are on either side of her.

ALICE
How did they get here? Well, there can be no harm in asking if the game is over. [*To the Red Queen*] Please, would you tell me –

RED QUEEN
Speak when you're spoken to!

ALICE
But if everybody obeyed that rule, and if you only spoke

when you were spoken to, and the other person always waited for *you* to begin, you see nobody would ever say anything, so that –

RED QUEEN

Ridiculous! Why, don't you see, child... [*Pause*] What on earth did you mean there a while back when you said 'and if I really am a Queen?' What right have you to call yourself so? You can't be a Queen till you've passed the proper examination. And the sooner we begin it the better.

ALICE   [*Piteous tone*]
I only said 'if'!

RED QUEEN   [*With shudder*]
She *says* she only said 'if' –

WHITE QUEEN   [*Moaning and wringing her hands*]
But she said a great deal more than that! Oh, ever so much more than that!

RED QUEEN

So you did, you know. Always speak the truth – think before you speak – and write it down afterwards.

ALICE
I'm sure I didn't mean –

RED QUEEN

That's just what I complain of! You should have meant! What do you suppose is the use of a child without any meaning? Even a joke should have some meaning – and a child's more important than a joke, I hope. You couldn't deny that, even if you tried with both hands.

ALICE
I *don't* deny things with my *hands*.

RED QUEEN
Nobody said you did. I said you couldn't if you tried.

WHITE QUEEN
She's in that state of mind that she wants to deny *some-thing* – only she doesn't know what to deny!

RED QUEEN
A nasty, vicious temper. [*Pause; to White Queen*] I invite you to Alice's dinner-party this afternoon.

WHITE QUEEN [*Smiling feebly*]
And I invite you.

ALICE
I didn't know I was to have a party at all, but, if there *is* to be one, I think *I* ought to invite the guests.

RED QUEEN
We gave you the opportunity of doing it, but I daresay you've not had many lessons in manners yet?

ALICE
Manners are not taught in lessons. Lessons teach you to do sums, and things of that sort.

WHITE QUEEN
Can you do Additions? What's one and one and one and one and one and one and one and one and one and one?

ALICE
I don't know. I lost count.

RED QUEEN
She can't do Addition. Can you do Subtraction? Take nine from eight.

ALICE
Nine from eight I can't, you know, but –

RED QUEEN
She can't do Subtraction. Can you do Division? Divide a
loaf by a knife – what's the answer to *that*?

ALICE
I suppose –

RED QUEEN
Bread-and-butter, of course.
Try another Subtraction sum.
Take a bone from a dog: what remains?

ALICE
The bone wouldn't remain, of course, if I took it – and the
dog wouldn't remain: it would come to bite me – and I'm
sure I shouldn't remain!

RED QUEEN
Then you think nothing would remain?

ALICE
I think that's the answer.

RED QUEEN
Wrong, as usual – the dog's temper would remain.

ALICE
But, I don't see how –

RED QUEEN
Why, look here! The dog would lose its temper, wouldn't
it?

ALICE
Perhaps it would.

RED QUEEN
Then if the dog went away, its temper would remain!

ALICE
They might go different ways. [*Aside*] What dreadful nonsense we *are* talking.

BOTH QUEENS
She can't do sums a *bit*!

ALICE [*Turning to White Queen*]
Can you do sums?!

WHITE QUEEN [*Gasping, shutting eyes*]
I can do Addition, if you give me time – but I can't do Subtraction under any circumstances! Do you know Languages? What's the French for fiddle-de-dee?

ALICE
[*Gravely*]
Fiddle-de-dee's not English.

RED QUEEN
Whoever said it was?

ALICE
[*Pause*]
If you'll tell me what language 'fiddle-de-dee' is, I'll tell you the French for it!

RED QUEEN
Queens never make bargains.

Suddenly, Alice is standing before the arched doorway: 'Queen Alice!' in large letters over it, with two bell handles – 'Visitors' Bell' and 'Servants' Bell.' Red and White Queen disappear behind the door from which crowd sounds emerge, muffled, then silence, then the Red Queen's shrill voice. Alice knocks on the door which is flung open – jarring hinge sounds.

RED QUEEN *in shrill voice (tune: 'Bonnie Dundee')*
To the Looking-Glass world
To the Looking-Glass world
To the Looking-Glass world it was Alice that said
'I've a sceptre in hand, I've a crown on my head.
Let the Looking-Glass creatures, whatever they be
Come and dine with the Red Queen,
  the White Queen, and me!'

ALL
Come and dine with the Red Queen,
  the White Queen, and me!

CHORUS
Then fill up the glasses as quick as you can,
And sprinkle the table with buttons and bran:
Put cats in the coffee, and mice in the tea –
And welcome Queen Alice with thirty-times-three!

Then fill up the glasses with treacle and ink
Or anything else that is pleasant to drink
Mix sand with the cider, and wool with the wine
And welcome Queen Alice with ninety times nine!

ALICE Thirty times three makes ninety. Oh, that'll never be done! I'd better go in at once.

14. Alice's Dinner Party

As she goes in, there is dead silence at the banquet table, around which sit all the Looking-glass creatures. Carroll mentions flowers which will take our memories back to the beginning of the show. There should be majestic special effect candles capable of growing very tall. Alice does quite a long and impressive walk during the silence to her chair between the Red and White Queens.

RED QUEEN [*Pause as Alice sits down*]
You've missed the soup and fish. Put on the joint!

Waiters set a leg of mutton before Alice.

RED QUEEN
You look a little shy: let me introduce you to that leg of mutton. Alice – Mutton: Mutton – Alice.

Each bows to the other.

ALICE [*Pause, then she cuts a slice, hands it to Red Queen*]
May I give you a slice?

RED QUEEN
Certainly not. It isn't etiquette to cut any one you've been introduced to. Remove the joint!

Waiters carry it off, bring on pudding – a large plum one.

ALICE
I won't be introduced to the pudding, please, or we shall get no dinner at all. May I give you some?

RED QUEEN [*Sulkily*]
Pudding – Alice: Alice – Pudding. Remove the pudding!

Pudding bows; waiters take it away.

ALICE
Waiter! Bring back the pudding!   [*Pause, she cuts a slice, hands it to Red Queen*]

PUDDING [*In thick suety voice*]
What impertinence! I wonder how you'd like it, if I were to cut a slice out of *you*, you creature!

RED QUEEN
Make a remark. It's ridiculous to leave all the conversation to the pudding! Remove the pudding.

ALICE [*Dead silence, pause, breathless attention*]
Do you know, I've had such a quantity of poetry repeated to me to-day. And it's a very curious thing. I think – every poem was about fishes in some way. Do you know why they're so fond of fishes, all about here?

RED QUEEN [*Slowly and solemnly, mouth close to Alice's ear*]
As to fishes, her White Majesty knows a lovely riddle – all in poetry – all about fishes. Shall she repeat it?

WHITE QUEEN [*Cooingly, close to Alice's other ear*]
Her Red Majesty's very kind to mention it. It would be *such* a treat! May I?

ALICE
Please do.

WHITE QUEEN [*Laughing, stroking Alice's cheek*]
   'First, the fish must be caught.'

CHORUS
That is easy:
a baby, I think, could have caught it.

WHITE QUEEN
  'Next, the fish must be bought.'

CHORUS
That is easy:
a penny, I think, would have bought it.

WHITE QUEEN
  'Now cook me the fish!'

RED QUEEN
That is easy, and will not take more than a minute.

WHITE QUEEN
  'Let it lie in a dish!'

CHORUS
That is easy, because it already is in it.

WHITE QUEEN
  'Bring it here! Let me sup!'

CHORUS
It is easy to set such a dish on the table.

WHITE QUEEN
  'Take the dish-cover up!'

CHORUS
Ah, *that* is so hard that I fear I'm unable!

WHITE QUEEN
  For it holds it like glue –

CHORUS
Holds the lid to the dish, while it lies in the middle:

WHITE QUEEN
Which is easiest to do,

CHORUS
Un-dish-cover the fish, or dishcover the riddle?

RED QUEEN
Take a minute to think about it, and then guess. Mean-while, we'll drink your health. [*Screaming at the top of her voice*] Queen Alice's health!

CHORUS
Queen Alice's health!

Some turn their glasses upside down on their heads; others pour out the decanters and lick up the wine as it dribbles off the table and others gurgle-guggle wine directly from bottles and small tuns. This accompanied by a fantasia of slurpy drink sounds; trickles, gurgles, as if we are now surfacing in the waters of the Looking-glass again.

ALICE [*Aside*]
Just like pigs in a trough.

RED QUEEN [*Frowning*]
You ought to return thanks in a neat speech.

WHITE QUEEN
We must support you, you know.

The Queens press close to stiffen her arms and lift her by these. Jabberwock's head with grin floats large above the chaos!

ALICE [*Whispering*]
Thank you very much, but I can do quite well without.

RED QUEEN
That wouldn't be at all the thing.

They lift her up into the air. Dead silence.

ALICE
I rise to return thanks –

WHITE QUEEN
Take care of yourself! Something's going to happen.

The candles shoot up in height to the ceiling, spouting fireworks sparks. Bottles fly about with plates as wings. Hoarse laugh at Alice's side: the leg of mutton is sitting beside her, not the White Queen. A soup-tureen lid flies up, or at least lifts up, to reveal the White Queen's head saying:

WHITE QUEEN
Here I am! [*Grins, then lets down the lid. The sounds accompanying this phantasmagoria should be explosive, fire-crackery, clatter of silver, ceramic, and glass, the hoarse laugh of the leg of mutton distorts and repeats, we hear the paddling of the White Queen inside the soup tureen; 'dreadful confusion', juicy sounds of a mind in nightmare as guests lie down to sleep in dishes.*]

ALICE [*Jumping up and grabbing the table cloth*]
I can't stand this any longer!

With great, heroic effort, she brings the whole phantasmagoria crashing to the floor. On the reflecting surface of the table or on the floor, now bare, a small Red Queen runs about, the size of a little girl, running after her shawl, which she trails after her, 'merrily,' like a kitten chasing its tail.

Alice turns first to where the Red Queen had been sitting and says:

ALICE
And as for *you* –

Then it is like catching a mouse, the doll leaping over a bottle that comes rolling down the table length. Lengthen this chase of a kitten-mouse to taste.

ALICE
As for *you,* I consider you to be the cause of all this mischief. I'll shake you into a kitten, that I will.

15. The Return!

Alice takes the Queen from the table, walks over as chaos lies defeated behind her, through dim light, almost unnoticed, to where the story began with her holding the kitten up as she sat on the carpet. The Red Queen made no resistance whatever; only her face grew very small, and her eyes got large and green. And still, as Alice went on shaking her, she kept on growing shorter – and fatter – and softer – and rounder – and – it really was *a kitten, after all.*

ALICE
Your Red Majesty shouldn't purr so loud. [*Laughing*] You woke me out of oh! such a nice dream! And you've been along with me, Kitty – all through the Looking-glass world. Did you know it, dear?

Kitten purrs as after a moment Alice searches about for the Red Queen chess piece by the hearth. She puts the kitten and the queen to look at each other.

ALICE
Confess that this was what you turned into.

The kitten turns away its head.

ALICE
Sit up a little more stiffly, dear! And curtsey while you're thinking what to – what to purr. It saves time, remember! [*Kisses the kitten*] Just in honour of your having been a Red Queen.

By the way, Kitty, if only you'd been really with me in my dream, there was one thing you *would* have enjoyed – I had such a quantity of poetry said to me, all about fishes.

Tomorrow morning, you shall have a real treat. All the time you're eating your breakfast, I'll repeat 'The Walrus and the Carpenter' to you; and then you can make believe it's oysters, dear!

Now, Kitty, let's consider who it was that dreamed it all.

Alice gets up and holds the kitten up to the Looking-glass. As before we see the reflection girl raising a reflection kitten.

ALICE
This is a serious question, my dear, and you should *not* go on licking your paw like that. You see, Kitty, it must have been either me or the Red King. He was part of my dream, of course – but then I was part of his dream, too! *Was* it the Red King, Kitty? You were his wife, my dear, so you ought to know – Oh, Kitty, *do* help to settle it! I'm sure your paw can wait!

We should hear the whistle of the Looking-glass train. As the light fades, the white snow and crimson fire effects intensify.

MEMBERS OF THE COMPANY
But the provoking kitten only began on the other paw, and pretended it hadn't heard the question.
Which do *you* think it was?

Only a purring sound replies.

THE END

Some Notes on the Text

PAGE 2: This Tenniel portrait of the Jabberwocky in all his horrible splendour is what Carroll originally intended for the frontispiece of *Through the Looking-Glass and What Alice Found There*, but, after consulting with thirty mothers, all of whom thought it much too frightening, he chose instead the portrait of Alice and the White Knight. After *Jurassic Park*, who nowadays would be scared of a mere Jabberwock?

PAGE 16: The chess game Carroll records for us here is not chess as we know it today. In India, where the game was first invented, the players would throw dice, and the number that the dice showed would be the number of squares you could take in your next move; this might explain why the white pieces are able to make so many continuous moves without waiting for Red to play. Despite that difference, it's still well worth while playing through the game Carroll describes as the chess version of his fantasy, using the eight pieces indicated in his diagram. Actually, what you will be playing is an end-game, and as you keep the story in mind you can actually see on the chess board the White Queen flying after her shawl (Move 2) and running away from the Red Knight when he attacks both her and the White King in a fork attack (Move 6). Children have asked me who the players of this chess game are and my answer is: Alice and her older sister. 'Because when we were playing just now' says Alice to the Black Kitten in the opening pages of the story. Alice evidently lost that game after making an unsuccessful check, when her sister's 'nasty' knight 'came wriggling down among my pieces' and very probably made a successful fork attack on her White Queen and White King. Then, in the dream of visiting Looking-glass House, Alice gets a chance to re-play the game. The 'nasty' Red Knight's attack on her is repelled by the White Knight and she becomes a Queen where her first act is to checkmate the Red King.
   Actors have also asked me why Alice gets by the Red King who

should be able to take her prisoner on White Queen 3. The answer is, first, that she flies over that square on a train. A pawn can, if it wants to, take two squares for its very first move. Still there is a law that says the Red King can then take her *en passant* (in flight) but he is asleep (Alice's sister may not have noticed) and Alice lands on a square protected by the White Knight who, remember, is also the author Lewis Carroll. You have to stay awake when you're playing chess or you may miss an opportunity to win the game! After Alice has changed her losing into winning in her wish-fulfilment dream, she can then wake up feeling quite happy and serene.

Lewis Carroll had been teaching the Liddell children how to play chess and another point to be made about the chess aspects of the story is that the actual game played in the story echoes those instruction books where you start with a simplified end-game first. As well, children catch on to the reason for all the split-second changes of place in the story before their slower parents; every chess move means the landscape changes in the twinkling of an eye.

PAGE 30: When Larkspur says: 'She's coming. I can hear her ... thump, thump, along the gravel-walk,' Carroll is poking fun at Lord Alfred Tennyson's *Maud*, a dramatic poem in which a depressed young man implores the beautiful, young Maud (how unlike that old battleaxe, the Red Queen) to 'come into the garden.' The thump-thump sound as the Red Queen does so results from her only having a pedestal to walk with so she must hop-hop wherever she goes. Victorian children and their parents would enjoy the ludicrous echo the Red Queen's foot-sounds make when they recalled that Tennyson's fair one had 'None like her, none./ Just now the dry-tongued laurels' pattering walk/ Seem'd her light foot along the garden walk ...'

PAGE 37 (and others): The sound of the 'brook' is heard each time that Alice is about to move to the next square. Carroll makes reference to 'six little brooks', which are actually the six horizontal lines which separate each set of squares on the chess board. Every time we hear the sound of the water, we realize that Alice is about to move forward to another stage on her journey towards becoming a Queen.

PAGE 71: *Jabberwocky* parodies Anglo-Saxon poetry, particularly the famous horror passage in *Beowulf* where the monster named Grendel comes in the night to attack Hart Hall, 'came striding in the dark night the shadow-goer' (cōm on wanre night/ scrīthan sceadugenga) 'The Jabberwock ... Came whiffling through the tulgey wood' sends up the earlier monster's 'scrīthan'. Since there is evidence that the chess people have read *Jabberwocky* – the White King mentions a brother monster called the Bandersnatch – and that they can read it backwards, this may explain some of the strange ways they talk as well as Hatta and Haigha's Anglo-Saxon attitudes.

PAGE 77: Humpy Dumpty seems to be in part a take-off on Alice's father, Dean Liddell of Christ Church College and the author of a famous Greek lexicon. He had the reputation of eating words for breakfast, an activity which Humpty also exhibits, as well as tendencies to academic fascism apparent in the Big Egg's famous retort to Alice's 'The question is whether you can make words mean so many different things.' To which Humpty (Dean Liddell as well?) replies: 'The question is which is to be master – that's all.' Eventually, the Liddell parents became quite sick of Carroll and asked him to cease visiting their home.

PAGE 107: Perhaps that is why the White Knight, who is Carroll's vision of his ageing self, and Alice can only meet in the forest of Square Seven where he sings her a parody of Wordsworth's *Resolution and Independence*. In this famous poem, the poet, while walking on the moors '... saw a Man before me unawares: /The oldest man he seemed that ever wore gray hairs.' 'What occupation do you there pursue,' asks the poet, observing the old man stirring a nearby puddle with a stick. Well, the answer is that the old man makes his living collecting leeches for the medical trade! After pondering this a while, the poet again asks, and this is what stirred up Carroll's sense of ridicule: 'How is it that you live, and what is it you do?' The poor old creature had just told Wordsworth, but the latter must needs get it out of him again. Patiently, the old leech-gatherer does a repeat and, eventually, his tormentor lets him be – without paying him anything for having extracted, despite the criticisms Carroll is making, a very fine poem from him. Carroll slyly implies this in the several times his Old Man tries to get a tip out of the White Knight – and utterly fails. Carroll's mind is too comic and sharp for romanticism, and perhaps he is also saying that it's all very well to idealize old peasants but what about putting your money as well as your sympathy on the counter.

A BOOK CALLED *Annotated Alice* is your best bet if you need more explanations. Right now, the solution to things you don't quite understand is to let the action of the story clarify them for you; in other words, just hang on. You'll dream about Alice tonight and then you'll understand everything at breakfast the next day because your subconscious has unravelled it for you. Meanwhile, don't be fooled by the fact that Carroll is known as a nonsense author. If so, why is he one of the world's most quoted authors? As Alice says about *Jabberwocky*, 'It's rather hard to understand! ... Somehow it seems to fill my head with ideas ... Only I don't exactly know what they are!' May you never know! For the fun of *Looking-glass*, with its riveting fantasy and incredible humour, is its infinite ability to suggest and suggest other possibilities without end.

To finish up, let's look at something Alice says to the White Kitten at the very end of the story – in the book, not the play; we couldn't find room for it.

'Snowdrop, my pet!' she went on, looking over her shoulder at the White Kitten, which was still patiently undergoing its toilet, 'when *will* Dinah have finished with your White Majesty, I wonder? That must be the reason you were so untidy in my dream. — Dinah! Do you know that you're scrubbing a White Queen? Really, it's most disrespectful of you!'

Here Carroll gives us a hint as to the relation between what was happening just before Alice went through the Looking-glass and what she then dreamed about in the split second she spent having that dream. She had already cast the black kitten as the Red Queen – for its energy and refusal to obey any other impulses than its own. The white kitten submitting to Dinah's vigorous cleaning became the White Queen, whose fur is also untidy and shawl always askew. Accordingly, the White Queen is passive, suffering, seems to speak in cooing mews and, in her running ability, reminds one of a cat pursued by a dog – in this case, the Red Knight. 'There's some enemy after her, no doubt,' says her husband. Why does she then become a sheep? Because in real life, Dinah does eventually make the white kitten into a *smoother* cat, all the wild sticking-out-fur as smooth as that of the Sheep in the Shop! Now, Alice takes a further step:

> 'And what did *Dinah* turn to, I wonder?.... Tell me, Dinah, did you turn to Humpty Dumpty? I *think* you did – however, you'd better not mention it to your friends just yet, for I'm not sure.'

On reflection,
the reason why Dinah
is Humpty Dumpty,
is that her white,
egg-shaped brow
(see the accompanying
Tenniel illustration)
appears in the shop
not far away from
the White Kitten/Sheep.
As Alice walks
toward this egg
which she has bought
from the Sheep,
it turns into
Humpty Dumpty.

The same situation occurs at the end of *Alice in Wonderland* when Alice's sister realizes that after Alice has told her dream to her

> ... she half believed herself in Wonderland, though she knew she had but to open them (her eyes) again, and all would change to dull reality – the grass would be only rustling in the wind (in the dream that was the White Rabbit running through the grass and down the rabbit-hole) the rattling teacups (of the Mad Hatter's tea-party) would change to tinkling sheep-bells, and the Queen's shrill cries to the voice of the shepherd boy – and the sneeze of the baby and all the other queer noises in Wonderland would change to the confused clamour of the busy farm-yard – while the lowing of the cattle in the distance would take the place of the Mock Turtle's heavy sobs.

What both the *Wonderland* and *Looking-glass* books imply, is that there is another level of consciousness altogether different from the one with which we see only 'dull reality'. Who knows what is really going on around us? Perhaps those two kittens and their mother really live in some other world where they are royalty and we ourselves have the chance to journey with Alice to a castle where we too will be crowned.

Is There Life After Alice?

That is, after you've seen the show, what do you do when you get home? Well, Elizabethan kids, in the days of Shakespeare, went home and tried to put on some of the scenes they'd witnessed at the Globe Theatre. I regret to say that these were usually the execution scenes. With these, Elizabethan producers had a marvellous trick where it looked as if someone had actually had their head chopped off – stage blood, severed head, headless corpse and all – the sort of Guignolesque horrors we complain about in today's violent ketchup movies. And there are records of sixteenth-century children spending hours in figuring out how the effect was accomplished.

However, we're dealing with a much, much gentler sort of story where the magic tricks involve, say, the March Hare's bag which seems capable of containing not only ham sandwiches and hay, but also a plum cake visibly much larger than the bag it comes out of: 'How they all came out of it Alice couldn't guess. It was just like a conjuring-trick, she thought.' Now, Lewis Carroll was a practitioner of magic tricks himself and a child's ability to glide through the mirror over a fireplace would have presented him with no problem. Speaking of his attitude to violence, he seems to keep it off stage; we never see the beheadings so often promised in *Wonderland* by the Red Queen, and indeed they never occur. In *Looking-Glass*, the White King does say to the unicorn that he needn't have passed his horn right through the Lion! However, the Unicorn replies: 'It didn't hurt him,' and, indeed, the Lion walks on just after this not visibly the worse for wear.

Magic tricks aside, unless you have a magician's handbook, my first notion of what you can do with the story as your own play is to borrow a chess set from your parents

The Imperial Kitten, Lily, and her Parents

and guardians and dress the pieces with the paper cut-outs we have provided you with at the end of this book. Or if a chess set is not available, saw up a dead tree branch into three-inch and two-inch sections (the latter for the pawns) and proceed as if with the chess pieces. You need to make sure the bottoms of these tree branch chess pieces are smooth and level or they won't stand up properly. As you can see from the photo, I haven't cut along the outlines of the figures, but made sure there's lots of paper, enough to wrap around the chess piece and fasten thereto with an elastic band wound round more than once to make it tight. Use the cast list Carroll himself made for a chess version. I found that painting the knight piece washably red (in my set he's black) or tying a red ribbon around him was enough of a costume; with the White Knight, I simply put the bare piece on the board. With their visors up, the two knights more or less look identical with their chess-piece selves. Bare pawns will do for the oysters and for the flower pawns; I cut out red and white daisy ruffs for the pawns involved, used orange paper for the Tiger Lily pawn, pink paper for the Rose one. Since Tenniel hasn't provided us with a crow, I cut one out from black paper and attached it to the black King's Bishop. Don't be afraid to include part, or even all, of another figure with your cutting out. In the case of the Old Man, you thereby get a chance to show the White Knight shaking him, and in the case of the Red King, you can show him with his Queen or some of her, or show him asleep, which you might not want to do until later on. The pawns should be shorter than the first row figures, so fold the figures we give you in half. I know there's a Lily pawn in Carroll's casting. Her mother calls her the Imperial kitten, but since Alice takes over her role, I took a Queen from another set I found, and an Alice from the *Wonderland* illustrations.

Possibly the best way to put on selected scenes, and they should be shortened down to five minutes each, all depending on what the traffic will bear, is to keep the

James Reaney leading an *Alice* workshop.

whole cast on a board of its own and draw or find another checker board for performance of the story. Suit yourself about setting this 'stage' board up the way Carroll indicates on page 16, but I think it helps to show your Alice as slowly but steadily proceeding across the board from Square Two to Square Eight, where she is crowned. You'll need a narrator who can fill gaps with pieces of the story – not so easy to do – particularly such scenes as the train scene and those involving drummers and soldiers. Everyone on stage for the last banquet scene; outdoors, under strict supervision, you might have firecrackers for the candles when the whole scene becomes very nightmarish and Alice is waking up. I'd use real kittens for the opening and the closing. A toy train for the Square Three scene might be fun, with someone telling who is on the train; Carroll hasn't cast chess pieces for Goat and Gentlemen in White paper et al. This is drama for the home and there's lots of room for improvisation; have some rehearsals though, because older people tend to wear out after the first quarter of an hour. On the other hand, you may be putting on the whole story just for yourself!

Moving up the scale from chess and toy theatre, let's look at Barbie dolls. At Stratford Collegiate, in the course of some workshops in January 1994, some writing students were in charge of producing miniaturized versions of scenes from *Looking-Glass*. In the case of the Garden of Live Flowers, one young woman used a recostumed Barbie as Alice, and for the flowers had her assistants hold up paper flowers she had made. They sat at a card table with a chess board and did a five-minute version – completely delightful and hilarious. I don't quite see Ken as the White Knight, but if you wrapped him in tinfoil with the cut-out, he might pass muster. For the mirror scenes you might choose two Barbie dolls identically dressed. Alice believes there is someone in Looking-glass House who holds up books when she does! And there is real shock value in her holding up the black kitten to the mirror and what does

An improvised Jabberwock.

the other girl hold up? Well, the Red Queen! We're on the edge of puppets and marionettes here, but the very fact that dolls can't move very much but their holders' arms can, gives that sort of a presentation immense charms. Investigate the local Sally Ann or Goodwill for used toys and dolls that might fill out your cast here. Always remember that in this kind of production you don't need an expensive mirror, all you need is the frame of a mirror.

We now come to what could happen in the gymnatorium of a public or high school where on the floor a chess board has been taped out or projected from a gobo on the ceiling above. The audience should sit on raised bleachers as at a basketball game. If you see the scenario suggested by Lewis Carroll's own chess diagram (see page 16) then you are more or less following the home version with chess actors. It's a Living Chess Game version, and you might want to investigate the Sadlers Wells ballet *Checkmate* for music and movement ideas. Along with this presentation, there might be a course on playing chess with a celebratory chess tournament. The various ways chess pieces move can be a lot of fun. I always remember Ray Bolger's ecstatic slide in *Where's Charley* as the model for the White Queen's entry. Since it involves at least thirty-two characters, this version is ideal for a school show, and for the very big scenes – Train, Drummer, Soldiers – bring on the cadet corps or the swimming team. The stylization problems are immense though and have to be worked out quite carefully.

Even more so, when you glance at the chess version published in the *British Chess Magazine* in 1887. The casting here is somewhat different from Carroll's and the story has been pulverized in order to fit in with a 'correct' chess game. At the Collegiate workshops already mentioned, there wasn't enough time to give this Bird's Opening *Looking-Glass* a complete try, but what I did remark was how early the slaughter of the Oyster pawns took place: '(d) Another Oyster comes up and is eaten'! I can see

Working through the script.

the reason why. There has to be an early extermination of pawns in order to clear the deck for the last scenes. The question is 'Why do this at all?' and the answer is: 'Because it's there!' Fair enough, but if you do try, exchange the designations of Pieces and Pawns for the Red side. One use for this version might be to do it as a dance prelude, swiftly executed for the more conventional chess version using Carroll's arrangement. Actually, the movement of the chess pieces in this version can be quite riveting, particularly if pieces react to their often quite unexpected deaths.

Another possibility is letting in more of the Victorian background, including the biography of the author. I once saw an English version long ago at the International Cinema in Toronto where Queen Victoria was on a visit to Oxford and was also commanding head-choppings right and left. Or –? There are many other possibilities.

Once when I was eight, I had a parallel experience to the one you may have just had, of watching a professional production, authentically acted with exuberance and supported by sophisticated design and fabulous illusions and compelling direction. My theatrical experience wasn't a play though. In those days, Stratford was not as lucky as it is nowadays, but what it was *was* my very first circus – Ringling Brothers – an absolutely enthralling show, unforgettably enchanting. The only reaction you could have was to go home and put on your own circus, in this case with my cousins and whatever the farm could muster. Cows as elephants? Of course, you couldn't rival the production you had just seen, but what you could do was with your own simplicity rival its feeling, and the attempt turned me into an artist. I don't see this as an improbable effect of the show you have just seen and I hope that the various first steps I have described in paralleling its effects and impacts may lead some of you to a lasting love of theatre and art.

The Alice Chess Game *

It is evident that Dodgson (Lewis Carroll) himself was not entirely satisfied with this solution, from his preface of 1896, as follows: –

As the chess problem, given on a previous page [see p 16], has puzzled some of my readers, it may be well to explain that it is correctly worked out, as far as the moves are concerned. The alternation of Red and White is perhaps not so strictly observed as it might be, and the 'Castling' of the three Queens is merely a way of saying that they entered the palace: but the 'check' of the White King at move 6, the capture of the Red Knight at move 7, and the final 'checkmate' of the Red King will be found, by any one who will take the trouble to set the pieces and play the moves as directed, to be strictly in accordance with the laws of the game.

We are inclined to agree with him as to 'alternation', for White takes eight moves in succession, enough to wipe out the entire Red force, which is scarcely to be called Chess, while the above play is not 'Alice', because a large number of the characters she meets in the book are not to be found on the board, while according to the alignment of men given under the heading of 'Dramatis Personæ' it is evident that two Oysters, the Red Bishops' Pawns, were eaten by their own comrades-in-arms, the Red Queen's Knight and Bishop.

Because of the above considerations, the following game has been prepared, which will be found fair chess; it is at least absolutely correct mechanically, while except

---

* From *The British Chess Magazine*, May 1910. Vol. 30, p. 181.

for one or two unimportant omissions, such as the meeting with the queer railway passengers, it reproduces the entire story.

We may remind the reader whose remembrance of 'Alice' is somewhat dim, that the 'Red Queen' furnishes Alice her Baedeker. 'You can be the White Queen's Pawn, if you like.' 'A Pawn goes two squares in its first move, you know. So you'll go very quickly through the third square, by railway, I would think – and you'll find yourself in the fourth square in no time. Well, that square belongs to Tweedledum and Tweedledee – the fifth is mostly water. The Sixth belongs to Humpty Dumpty; the Seventh Square is all forest. However, one of the Knights will show you the way, and in the Eighth Square we shall all be Queens together.' We have also attempted to work in the incidental references of the book, even to Tweedledum's 'If that there King was to wake, you'd go out – bang! – just like a candle.'

DRAMATIS PERSONAE *

WHITE		RED	
Pieces	*Pawns*	*Pawns*	*Pieces*
Tweedledee	Fish	Frog	Unicorn
Lion	Haigha	Messenger	Carpenter
Sheep	Fish	Daisy (a)	Walrus
White Queen	Alice	Tiger Lily (a)	Red Queen
White King	Hatta	Rose (a)	Red King
Aged Man (b)	Oyster	Fawn	Crow
White Knight (b)	Oyster	Violet (a)	Red Knight
Tweedledum	Oyster	Daisy (a)	Humpty Dumpty

---

* This array of chess pieces differs somewhat from the array used in the Stratford production.

WHITE	RED	WHITE	RED
1 P – K B 4	1 P – Q 4	34 Q – Q 3 (n)	34 B – R 5 (o)
2 P – K 3	2 P – K 3	35 Kt – R 5	35 Q R – Q B sq
3 Kt – K B 3	3 Kt – K B 3	36 P – Q 5	36 B – B 2
4 B – Q 3	4 P – Q B 4	37 Kt – B 4	37 P – K R 3
5 P – Q Kt 3	5 Kt – Q B 3	38 B – K 5 (p)	38 B – B 3
6 B – Q Kt 2	6 B – Q 3	39 B x B	39 Kt x B
7 P – Q B 4	7 Castles	40 Q – Q 4	40 Kt – R 2
8 Kt – Q B 3	8 P – Q Kt 3	41 P – B 5	41 Q – K 2
9 Kt – K 2	9 Q – B 2	42 P – Q 6 (q)	42 Q – B sq
10 P – Q R 3	10 K R – Q sq	43 Q x P ch	43 K – R sq
11 Q – Q B 2	11 P – K 4	44 Q – B 3	44 P – K R 4
12 P – B 5	12 P – K 5	45 Q – B 2	45 B – Kt sq
13 Kt – Kt 5	13 Q B x B P (c)	46 Kt – Kt 6	46 Q – Kt 2
14 B x P	14 P x B	47 Kt – K 7 (r)	47 R – Kt sq (s)
15 P – K Kt 4 (d)	15 B x P (d)	48 Kt x B	48 Q x Kt
16 Kt x K P	16 Kt – K sq	49 K – R 2	49 R – Kt 4
17 Q Kt – Kt 3	17 B – K 3	50 K – R 3	50 R – R 4 ch
18 Castles QR (e)	18 Kt – K 4	51 K – Kt 4	51 R – R 3
19 K R – Kt sq	19 Kt – Kt 5	52 R – Q 5	52 R – K B sq
20 Kt – R 5	20 Kt x R P (f)	53 R x P	53 R x R
21 Kt x Kt P	21 K – B sq	54 Q x R	54 R – B 3
22 R – Kt 2	22 Kt – B 6	55 P – K 4 (t)	55 R – B sq
23 Q R – K B sq	23 K – K 2	56 Q – Q 5 ch	56 K – Kt sq
24 R x Kt	24 P – Kt 4 (g)	57 P – K 5 (t)	57 Q – B sq
25 R – B sq	25 P – Kt 5 (g)	58 Kt – K 4 (t)	58 Q – Q sq
26 P x P	26 P x P	59 K – B 4	59 P – K R 5
27 Kt – B 5 ch	27 K – Q 2	60 P – Q 7	60 R – B 2
28 Kt (B5) – Kt 3	28 K – B 3	61 P – B 6	61 Kt – B sq (u)
29 R – Q sq	29 K B – K 2	62 Kt – B 6 (v)	62 P – R 6
30 Kt sq	30 Q – Q 2 (h)	63 Q – Q 6	63 Kt – Kt 3
31 P – Q 4 (i)	31 K – Kt 2 (j)	64 Kt – K 8	64 P – R 7
32 R (Kt 2) – Q 2 (k)		65 Kt x R	65 Q x Kt
	32 P – B 4 (l)	66 P – Q 8 (Q), and mate (w)	
33 Kt – B 2	33 B – Kt 4 (m)		

(a) The Red Queen's Garden.

(b) The meeting of the Aged Man and White Knight.

(c) The Walrus commences on the Oysters.

(d) Another Oyster comes up, and is eaten.

(e) Tweedledee steals Tweedledum's rattle – *i.e.*, the privilege of Castling.

(f) The Carpenter gets his share of the Oysters.

(g) Humpty Dumpty sends his Messenger to the Fish.

(h) Alice meets the Red Queen just before starting. (The Red Queen now commanding Alice's square).

(i) The Fourth Square by railway.

(j) The Red King is now where Alice will not disturb his slumbers.

(k) 'The Fourth Square belongs to Tweedledum and Tweedledee,' who now command it. The King's Messenger, Haigha, is in prison, his further advance being blocked.

(l) Alice meets the Fawn.

(m) The Crow frightens Tweedledum.

(n) Alice, on the Fourth Square, meets the White Queen.

(o) The Crow flies away.

(p) Alice, on the Fifth Square, meets the Sheep.

(q) Alice, on the Sixth Square, meets Humpty Dumpty.

(r) The Lion and the Unicorn fight.

(s) The Lion wins.

(t) The King sends his Soldiers and Messengers.

(u) Alice attacked by the Red Knight.

(v) And defended by the White.

(w) The Queens are having their party, the Red Queen most decidedly being in the soup.

In conclusion, I wish to acknowledge the helpful criticism of Mr. A. C. White.

DONALD M. LIDDELL

Acknowledgements

The cover illustration and drawings of the Walrus and Humpty Dumpty on pages 21 and 75 are reproduced courtesy of John Pennoyer, who designed the costumes for the 1994 Stratford production.

All of the pencil caricatures of the Stratford cast in rehearsal were drawn by James Reaney.

The Jabberwocky on page two, as well as the illustration of Alice with the cats on page 129 and all of the 'cut-outs', are by Sir John Tenniel as they appeared in the original (1872) Macmillan edition of *Through the Looking-Glass and what Alice found there.*

The workshop photographs on pages 136 and 138 were taken by Scott Wishart and are reproduced courtesy of the *Stratford Beacon Herald.*

The author photograph on the back cover, and the photograph of James Reaney with workshop participant on page 140, are reproduced courtesy of Scott Wishart.

Shown on page 149 is Eli Franken playing a mean game of chess. Eli is the son of Jerry Franken who toured the country as Jim Donnelly in 1975. This photograph is courtesy of Wilma McCaig.

Cut-outs to Make Your Own Chess Game

The suggested DRAMATIS PERSONAE listed below was devised by James Reaney through the course of his work in adapting *Alice Through the Looking-Glass* for the stage. To use the John Tenniel cut-outs that are provided, simply cut each rectangular piece on the dotted line, fold it over and tape the ends together on the dashed line and then slip the Looking-glass 'costumes' over the appropriate chess piece 'actors' (as pictured in the photograph on the previous page).* There are no cut-outs for the Crow, Red Knight or the flower and oyster pawns. You may wish to make your own cut-outs for the flowers (Daisy, Rose, etc.) from coloured paper and for the Crow using black paper while a plain pawn might work best for the oysters. A piece of red paper may suffice as costume for the Red Knight. For more instructions and ideas, refer to the text of the play and to the essay 'Is There Life After Alice?'.

DRAMATIS PERSONAE

WHITE		RED	
Pieces	*Pawns*	*Pawns*	*Pieces*
Tweedledee	Daisy	Daisy	Lion
Unicorn	Haigha	Messenger	Walrus
Sheep	Oyster	Oyster	Carpenter
White Queen	Alice	Tiger Lily	Red Queen
White King	Fawn	Rose	Red King
Aged Man	Oyster	Oyster	Crow
White Knight	Hatta	Frog	Red Knight
Tweedledum	Daisy	Daisy	Humpty Dumpty

---

* These 'costumes' are designed to fit best over one-inch diameter chess pieces.

WHITE ROOK - TWEEDLEDUM

WHITE KNIGHT

WHITE BISHOP - AGED MAN

WHITE KING

RED ROOK - HUMPTY DUMPTY

RED PAWN - MESSENGER

RED PAWN - FROG

RED KING

WHITE ROOK - TWEEDLEDEE

WHITE KNIGHT - UNICORN

WHITE BISHOP - SHEEP

WHITE QUEEN

RED ROOK – LION

RED KNIGHT – WALRUS

RED BISHOP – CARPENTER

RED QUEEN

WHITE PAWN - HATTA

WHITE PAWN - FAWN

WHITE PAWN - HAIGHA

WHITE PAWN - LILY - ALICE